KEYS TO
COLLEGE SUCCESS

Lilburn P. Hoehn
James E. Sayer
Wright State University

MAYFIELD PUBLISHING COMPANY
Mountain View, California

Library of Congress Cataloging-in-Publication Data

Sayer, James Edward.
   Keys to college success / Lilburn P. Hoehn, James E. Sayer.
      p. cm.
   Includes bibliographies and index.
   ISBN 0-87484-812-1
   1. Study, Method of. 2. College students—Time management.
3. Reading (Higher education) I. Hoehn, Lilburn P. II. Title.
LB2395.S28 1989
378′.17′02812—dc19   88-7574
                                       CIP

Manufactured in the United States of America
10 9 8 7 6 5 4 3 2

Mayfield Publishing Company
1240 Villa Street
Mountain View, California 94041

Sponsoring editor, Franklin C. Graham; production editor, Linda Toy; manuscript editor, Victoria Nelson; text designer, Juan Vargas; cover designer, Ingbritt Christensen. The text was set in 10/12 Garamond by Digitype and printed on 50# Finch Opaque by George Banta Company.

CONTENTS

TO THE STUDENT

The purpose of this book is to help you understand more about learning, improve your study skills, and develop the self-discipline you need to be a successful college student. Perhaps the goal of self-discipline is most important, for achieving it will benefit you not only in college but also in your career. While you are taking classes, it may seem that all you are doing is acquiring and demonstrating a knowledge of specific subjects. But you are accomplishing a lot more than that: while you are reading and listening, jotting notes, writing papers, and taking tests, you are also developing the skills and discipline to manage your time, to balance your work with family and other responsibilities—in short, to succeed both in and beyond college.

Of course, this book cannot develop skills and discipline for you; you must do that yourself. But you will find in these pages a concise, practical handbook full of ideas and experiences that you can immediately put to use. It is not a theoretical treatise; it offers simple, direct advice on how you can achieve academic success.

Each chapter begins with a list of learning objectives: that is, what you can gain from studying that chapter. Throughout the chapter, important points are strongly emphasized, and exercises and experiences are provided to make the material real for you. Each chapter concludes with review questions to help you remember the most important information.

Individual chapters (4 through 8) focus on the key skills of listening, notetaking, reading, writing, and taking exams—skills you obviously must develop for academic success. These are not all the keys to success, however. You also need to understand your motivation for being in college, to be able to deal with conflicts in your life, and to have personal habits that are productive. These matters are discussed in Chapter 1, The Savvy of Being a Student, which is followed by two chapters on the processes of learning and remembering. The final chapter (which you may wish to read earlier) focuses on how to manage your time.

We hope not only that you will find this book helpful but also that you will enjoy using it as much as we enjoyed writing it for you.

LPH
JES

THE SAVVY OF
BEING A STUDENT

$\bullet\ \bullet\ \bullet\ \bullet\ \bullet$

The authors of this book make two assumptions about you — the reader. The first is that you are already going to college or that you plan to enroll in college. The second is that you want to gain every advantage possible toward succeeding in college. The fact that you are reading a book like this one does not necessarily imply that you are or will have difficulty achieving success in college. The wise student — strong or mediocre — will actively seek to improve in those key areas that can lead to success.

The purpose, therefore, of this book is to provide you with various kinds of help in enhancing your abilities as a student, regardless of your entry level of expertise. Some benefits you may derive from reading and studying this book include the following:

1. *Learning strategies:* You will develop greater understanding of the psychology of learning and how you can get the most out of the learning process.

2. *Academic skill:* You will be able to improve those critical academic skills that facilitate learning in all areas. These are reading, listening, writing, note taking, and test taking.

3. *Study skills and habits:* You will be able to improve your study skills and habits through understanding your own learning processes and strengthening your academic skills.

4. *Personal management skills:* You will acquire ideas and techniques to manage important factors such as making decisions and using time effectively.

5. *Self-understanding:* You will gain greater self-understanding, especially in areas related to how you learn, make decisions, and function in general.

6. *Skills in solving everyday problems:* You will gain insight into dealing with those everyday problems that interfere with your primary mission — obtaining a college degree.

Each of these areas is treated in turn in this book though not to the same depth or in the same format. Academic skills, for example, are each covered in a separate chapter, whereas other items are discussed throughout the book. Suggested reading lists are provided if you wish to explore a given area beyond the material presented here.

WHAT IS SUCCESS?

Because we have introduced the notion of *success* in your role as a college student, it seems useful to examine that concept more closely. Measurement or perception of success is a highly subjective matter that depends on each person's own frame of reference. Some would judge Al Capone, the famous gangster of the twenties and thirties, for example, as successful because he had money, power, and control; others would rate him a failure because his actions were not socially acceptable. Success, however, ought to be judged on the extent to which a person attains his or her goal or goals within the realm of societal acceptability. Part of a college education consists of developing an ethical and value structure that will enhance your ability to succeed in life. Sometimes success in terms of money and power can be achieved via questionable ethics and values, but usually persons who choose that route end up with damaged reputations, smaller bank accounts, and loss of power: witness the altered lives of those involved in the Watergate scandal of the seventies. It is each person's responsibility to examine his or her ethics and values and to adjust these in a direction that will help achieve goals without employing negative means in reaching these ends.

A *goal* can be translated into a series of steps or *subgoals*, the attainment of which moves a person closer to a major goal. Usually, once a goal has been attained, it is time to set a new goal. Suppose, for example, you want to become the president of a computer software company that creates and markets computerized learning programs for college-level science and math courses. Suppose further that in ten years you want to capture 30 percent of the market with your product. Think about the steps or subgoals you would need to attain to reach your major goal. You would need a high level of knowledge about computers and software development as well as management, finances, personnel, and the like. How would you organize your formal education to attain each of these subgoals? Actually, within each of these subgoals are other subgoals, often referred to as *short-range objectives*. It is usually most productive to direct your energy toward the attainment of the smallest subgoal, or the short-range objectives; otherwise, you could end up like the baseball team that looks ahead to a series with the division leader but overlooks the series with the last-place club and loses two out of three to it. Your focus needs to be on the short-range objectives, arranged in a logical sequence.

Although it is not absolutely necessary to have a college degree to be president of your own computer software company, a degree is a valuable asset. Thus we define your first long-range goals as the college degree. Contained within that long-range goal are a number of short-range objectives, namely, successfully completing each course in your program. Therefore, success for you in terms of your current pursuit means completing each course leading to the degree, which in turn will help you to secure employment, which will help you begin to establish yourself, build a financial base — and on and on toward your major goal.

WHAT FACTORS RELATE TO YOUR SUCCESS?

A number of factors are related to your success as a college student. These include your motivation, intelligence, knowledge background, academic skills, study skills, personal management skills, experience, and the like. Some of these factors are academic, some are directly related to academics, and others are clearly not academic but indirectly relate to your success as a student. We will explore some of these factors in the remainder of this chapter.

Motivation

How important is motivation to success? Frequently, motivation is the crucial determinant of success for persons of both high and average intelligence. Too many people jump into their college careers without giving their leap sufficient thought. For many, going to college simply means the next logical step after high school. Some believe that college is their key to future vocational, financial, and social success. Still others decide to go to college because they cannot think of anything better to do.

Unfortunately, too many college students-to-be do not stop to ask themselves this important two-part question: (1) "Am I right for college?" and (2) "Is college right for me?" Instead, they plunge right into higher education without knowing why they are there—and, all too often, the final result is far from pleasant. Just because your mother and father went to college does not mean that *you* should go to college—even if your parents expect you to do so. Just because all your lifelong friends go to college does not mean that *you* should go to college—even if they put great pressure on you to join them. College is *not* right for everyone. Concomitantly, not everyone is right for college.

Making a decision to go to college is not the same as deciding to go to a movie on Friday night, although some people take the plunge just as casually, as the following exchange demonstrates.

MARK: What are you going to do next year?

DAVE: Well, I don't want to hang around home, and there's no job I'm interested in, so I think I'll go to college.

Dave is going to experience an unpleasant surprise, at least at first. Why? Because he has no real reason for going to college, only that he cannot see doing anything else. Now that might be an acceptable decision if college were only a weekend activity, over in two or three days, but college is much more than that. The standard or typical college degree program requires four years of full-time study during the fall, winter, and spring months. Certain programs, especially those that are technically based or contain field or "practicum" experiences, require either five years or summer study to complete degree requirements.

It is possible to attend college for the wrong reasons and succeed, but only about 25 percent of those who start to college actually receive a degree. One of the reasons some of these entrants never finish college is probably because they entered with the wrong motivation. As noted earlier, some go to college to have a good time; some because it is the thing to do; some because of parental or peer pressure; some to participate in sports; some because a friend is going; some to secure a pot of gold; others for a host of unnamed reasons. No one can say that any of those reasons is necessarily wrong if the student succeeds. Chances for success are lessened, however, if the motivation derives from any reason other than obtaining a college education.

The important thing is to be honest about your motivation. If one of the foregoing is your own primary reason for attending, admit it—at least to yourself. You may find that your reasons for going to college may not be sufficiently strong to see you through four years. You may wish to examine your motivation in an honest manner with someone who can take an objective position and help you explore your reasons for attending college. Even though your reasons may be sound at the beginning, you may question them at a later time—even after a year of success. To do so is probably positive if only to confirm your original decision, but you may also discover other factors that will enhance your motivation.

Perhaps you will seriously question why you are going to college or why you are attending the college where you are enrolled. These are legitimate questions and need to be addressed, if they come up, early in your college education rather than after four years of attendance. It may be that college in general is not for you or that the specific college you are attending is not for you. You may want to gain some work experience or spend two years in the military or some other endeavor and then return to college. You may feel another college—a larger or a smaller one, a rural or a city college, private or state—would be more appropriate for you. It is important, as you think about your motivation, that you also consider alternatives if you find your motivation flagging in your current situation.

It is possible, even likely, that your motivation will be strengthened if you function from a position of security. Some of this security can come from your intelligence or your knowledge, but some of it can come from your skills in learning and studying. Some useful techniques that can help you learn to read, study, write papers, and prepare for exams will be presented in later chapters.

Ask a few friends or classmates about their reasons for attending college. Their answers should provide you with at least two pieces of information. You may find that some don't know why they are there. You will also find that their motivation will vary. The important thing is to consider whether your own motivation is appropriate and strong enough to see you through four years of study.

Intelligence

Is intelligence related to success in college? The majority of educational psychologists would probably say that it is. Certainly, people of high intelligence have it easier in college as long as their motivation and drive are sufficient. What we don't know is the lower limit of measured intelligence necessary to do well in college. Some persons do well because of their high level of motivation, whereas others of higher intelligence may not succeed because of a low level of motivation. Discounting temporarily the influence of high or low motivation, there is still the problem of finding a means of measuring intelligence accurately. Note the following definitions.

1. "Intelligence is the disposition to behave intelligently through the organization and control of cognitive processes employed toward the solutions of problems which challenge the well-being, needs, plans and survival of the individual" (Charlesworth, 1976).

2. "A major aspect of intelligence is the ability to solve problems" (Resnick and Glaser, 1976).

3. "The definition of intelligence may become possible only after unitary structures have been discovered experimentally, but they can be discovered only from measurement research" (Cattell, 1971).

4. "The variability in the material presented leads me to conclude that . . . intelligence may be defined as what the participants report that they measure" (Voss, 1976).

Given the wide differences in these definitions, you can quickly surmise the difficulties in measuring intelligence, a task to which educators, psychologists and others have devoted countless hours. It is one thing to suggest that an individual is of high, average, or low intelligence but quite another to quantify minute differences within those categories. This is exactly what has been attempted by those researchers who have studied and attempted to measure and quantify that abstract quality we call "intelligence." Some have put so much faith in existing technology that decisions significantly affecting persons' lives have been and still are made on the basis of the few points between an individual's test score and some arbitrary cutoff point.

Intelligence test data have also been used to predict academic or occupational success. Some researchers believe that if a positive relationship between test scores and academic or occupational success can be found, tests can then be used to predict such success. Thus, persons could be counseled more effectively about some important choices. Even though such information can provide some indication of probable success, however, predictive accuracy is quite another matter. At best, a person's intelligence will probably not account for more than about 25 percent of the variance involved in academic or occupational success. Even if tests were accurate, it is still doubtful that predications of success could be made from the scores. Too many variables other than intelligence influence success.

Intelligence tests may also be inaccurate for other reasons. Cultural bias is usually present; indeed, it is very difficult to avoid given the multicultural, diverse population of these United States. Because tests are used for large groups throughout the country, they tend to be geared to white middle- and upper-class Americans. Thus, someone out of that mainstream culture may not perform well on the tests, which obviously makes predictions even more difficult. Individual performance on tests is also often a function of personal experiences such as breadth and depth of reading, travel, hobbies, and school subjects.

The point is that the necessary knowledge about intelligence and the technology to quantify it for accurate predictions of success do not exist. Yes, *some* knowledge and technology exist, but not to the degree of refinement that allows important decisions to be based solely on test data. *Therefore, we suggest to you that you may not want to pay much attention to those intelligence test scores someone may have given you, so long as you have strong motivation.*

Well, then, how important *is* intelligence to success in college? It's important but also probably overrated — in two ways. First, intelligence as described is usually determined by a test that may not accurately reflect this quality. Second, traditionalists feel that only bright persons should attend college, a belief perpetuated by elitists who don't stop to think about the other factors that enter into the success picture. Your intelligence is an indicator of your *probable* success in college. It is not a perfect predictor.

Background and Experience

Background and experience are most certainly related to success in college. As we use it here, *background* is the foundation you have in core areas such as English, math, the humanities, and the social and natural sciences, as well as the study skills and habits you have developed.

Subjects other than core or general education subjects are, of course, very important — perhaps more important to you — but most colleges and universities have a required core or general education program. Therefore, even though you may not be planning to major in one of the core areas, you need that solid foundation to succeed during your first year or so in college. Some students are highly interested in one subject area and find it difficult to generate the motivation and interest to succeed in other areas. In some ways this keen interest is commendable because it provides a focus and the possible motivation to accomplish something in that subject. Colleges and universities insist, however, — and justifiably — that you complete a core or general program that will help you become a broadly educated person. College instructors also assume that you have some kind of knowledge base when you enter college and therefore do not always start with the basics in courses. If you lack background in the basic courses, your success in college becomes more difficult.

Besides the background you have received through formal education, you can develop a knowledge background in various ways. One way to improve your background is to read many different kinds of material. Magazines such as *Time, Newsweek, U.S. News and World Report, Fortune, National Geographic*, and others are excellent materials for increasing both the breadth and depth of your knowledge. Novels provide another good source for increasing your general knowledge and vocabulary as well as for improving your imagination. Newspapers and television news programs and documentaries can expand your fund of general knowledge. In short, absorb as much information on as many topics as you can from as many outside sources as possible.

Obviously, not all your personal experiences will contribute to your success in college. It is probable, though, that a broad range of experience will give you a frame of reference useful for understanding and absorbing the content in your classes. Any time you are able to relate class content to your own experience, it becomes more meaningful. Try observing one or more students who are a few years older than the majority of students. As you listen to these students in class or talk to them outside class, see if you detect the effect of experience. You may also find that older students tend to make better grades or find learning easier. Some of that difference may come from motivation, but some of it may simply be because they have had the time to accumulate more personal experience.

THE SAVVY YOU NEED TO SUCCEED

Other than essential ingredients such as motivation, drive, intelligence, study skills and habits, and academic skills, you will need a fair amount of savvy to succeed in college. *Savvy* here means knowing how to get things accomplished—knowing your environment and how to use it.

The ideas in this book should help you with the study skills you need to help secure and use your knowledge base. The following sections will be focused on those factors not directly related to your program or your ability to study, write, take tests, and so on. These factors, however, have a definite impact on your success as a student. Overall, you need to know that a university is a complex social system that attempts to meet your needs in many ways other than the strictly academic. Academic needs represent your primary reason for being at a university, but understanding the support services of this institution is important to your overall success.

Savvy is . . .

knowing what the various *service and support offices* do and where they are located. Some of the indirect service or support offices you may need to know about are:

1. The registrar's office
2. The bursar's office
3. The financial aid office
4. The testing office
5. The counseling office
6. The placement office
7. The student employment office

Two direct support services can be very important to your success in college—the computer center and the library.

1. The computer center—that is, the facility with computers available for students—is becoming increasingly important to students' success in college. Microcomputers may be housed in various locations or perhaps in one large center. It is important that you know what is available for student use. You also need to know the software available and what help you can expect from the staff who works in the center.

2. The library is probably the service you will utilize with the greatest frequency—if you want to be a successful student, that is. The student with library savvy is often a successful student. What do you need to know about the library?

   - How to find the materials you need.
   - How to use the various reference services available.
   - How to check out a book.
   - Where books, journals, and other study materials are held in reserve.
   - How to use the various types of "micro" forms: microfiche and the like.
   - What to do if the book you need is not available.
   - The regulations related to journals and other material that can't be removed from the library.
   - How to do computer searches for materials.
   - Where the serious students hide in the library to study.

If you don't know how to use the library, there are usually library orientation classes available. Sign up for one—it will save you many wasted hours.

Savvy is . . .

knowing how to *deal with the conflicts* you face daily in both your academic and nonacademic life. Unless you are a hermit living in a cave, you will face conflictual situations in your life. Contrary to what some people believe, conflict is not necessarily a negative experience; on the contrary, it can be very growth producing. Typically, the negative factors and associated stress may be a result of the way you manage the conflict rather than of the conflict itself. Conflict can be functional or dysfunctional in terms of its possible outcome and the way that outcome is reached. *Functional conflict* simply means conflict that, when dealt with or managed properly, can help us solve problems and grow from the experience. Without functional conflict — that is, if everything merely ran smoothly in our lives — we would never grow dissatisfied and act to remove that dissatisfaction. Working to remove the dissatisfaction — in an appropriate manner — is what usually helps us grow. *Dysfunctional conflict* is conflict that does not produce growth. It is usually conflict that obstructs action or somehow interferes with reaching a solution or solving a problem.

The reason for bringing up this subject here is simply that conflict and its management and/or lack of management can have a serious effect on your success as a student. Stop and think now about the current conflictual situations you face. If you can't think of any, try differences with your girlfriend or boyfriend, parent, sibling, classmate, teacher, neighbor, school administrator, department store, rule or regulation, the Registrar's Office, and so on. Some people are so insensitive to those around them that they may not be affected by conflict — that is, conflict may *not* interfere with their functioning. Others, however — and this includes many of us — are unable to function as effectively when conflict of any magnitude is present in our lives.

Conflict can be classified by type and there are various ways of classifying. We will mention four types of conflicts as indicated by Frey (1979).

1. *Intrapersonal:* conflict you experience within yourself. (Example: You are angry with yourself because you flunked a test you did not study for and you feel some study could have made the difference.)

2. *Interpersonal:* conflict you experience with another person or with a group of people. (Example: You are angry with your roommate because he plays the radio too loud late at night while he studies.)

3. *Personal-organizational:* conflict you experience with an organization such as a university or a department store. (Example: You are irritated with a store where you bought an article of clothing because you were refused a refund.)

4. *Impersonal:* conflict you might experience with society or the environment. (Example: You are extremely upset because society is doing little to solve the drug abuse problem.)

Probably those types of conflicts are interrelated in various ways. If you have an intrapersonal conflict of some magnitude, it could easily spill over into your relations with friends or family so that interpersonal conflict is added. When a conflict begins to spill over into other classifications, it is obviously more difficult to manage appropriately. You might find it instructive to examine your own conflicts within the framework of these classifications. Are most of your conflicts of one type or do you experience conflict in all the types? It might be helpful to jot down a few of your present conflicts and see if they fall in one, two, or more categories.

There are a number of ways of managing conflict. Thomas and Kilman suggest five methods for managing conflict:

1. *Competing:* handling the conflict through competitive means so that somebody loses. (Example: You deal with a conflict with a boyfriend or girlfriend by going on a date with another person.)

2. *Collaborating:* working out a solution with the other person or persons involved. (Example: Two teenagers both want the car on Saturday night. They decide to double date.)

3. *Compromising:* bargaining or finding a middle ground so that no one wins and no one loses. (Example: One person wants to go to a concert and the other wants to go out for a nice dinner. Because funds are limited they can't do both, so they go to a movie and a fast food restaurant.)

4. *Avoiding:* staying away from situations where one knows or suspects that conflict can develop. (Example: Joe stays away from a meeting of the Ole Boys Club because Tom will be there and each time they are both at the meeting, interpersonal conflict develops.)

5. *Accommodating:* giving in or smoothing over so that some harmony exists at least on a temporary basis. (Example: A mother says, ''Now let's stop the bickering—you are brother and sister and you love each other.'')

How do you typically manage the conflict you face? Do you use various methods according to the nature of the conflict or the situation, or do you use the same management method for all your conflicts? Any of the methods given here can be appropriate and useful in some situations but disastrous in others. For example, Jane wants to resolve a difference with Mary, who is amenable to working out a solution by compromise. Each time they get together, however, Jane uses a competitive approach, which turns Mary off.

If an unresolved conflict prevents you from functioning at a high level of effectiveness, recognize that fact and do something about it. Think about the nature of the conflict and an appropriate management strategy. Try it and see what happens. Many strategies other than the five listed here are possible; another might appeal to you more. If you still have difficulty managing the conflict, discuss the problem with a trusted friend or, if it persists, see a counselor. Some time and energy invested in finding a solution may pay high dividends later.

Savvy is . . .

handling disappointments, setbacks, and failure in a productive manner. How do you respond when you receive a grade lower than you wanted on an exam or paper you have written? Do you blame the instructor for throwing you a curve ball on the test or for evaluating your paper unfairly? Do you mope around with a sad face, hoping someone will show sympathy for your condition? Do you try to learn from the disappointment or failure? Obviously, the latter represents the positive reaction, because such experiences can produce growth. The mental attitude you develop after a disappointment or failure can have a significant impact on your success as a student.

Certainly there are cases in which a high percentage of a class does poorly on an exam or an instructor evaluates tests or papers unfairly, using criteria not previously shared. In general, such cases represent the exception rather than the rule because the intent of most professors is to help you learn, not hinder you. Any time you receive a grade (midterm, final, course grade, term paper grade, etc.) lower than your expectation, you should ask certain questions: (1) Was my expectation too high? (2) Did I study enough and properly for the exam? (3) Was the paper well written or did I throw it together? Notice the questions all point to you, not to another person or to the situation. Whenever your performance is lower than your expectation, look inward first. The chances are good that you are part of the problem.

What can you do to learn from a disappointing or failing grade? First, develop the appropriate mental attitude: that you are part of the problem. We are not suggesting that you debase yourself or think about how bad you are, but simply that you accept the idea that the major responsibility for the situation belongs to you. Second, analyze the exam in terms of the errors you made. Did you simply not know some of the material? Was your thinking process fuzzy? Did you not know facts and details? Did you not know principles and concepts? Responding to questions such as these should help you get a handle on the type of adjustments you need to make. After failing a test, some students feel they must study harder for the next one. This may be true, but it is also important to determine the *type* of errors you made so that your studying can be directed more effectively.

Sometimes instructors do not return the test questions of objective tests, but only the answers and your score. This practice makes it difficult for you to analyze your performance in the terms just indicated. In such cases, ask the instructor for an appointment to look at the test questions yourself or to go over them with him or her. An exam should be a learning experience just as a lecture or reading the text is a learning experience. Without access to test questions, learning from your mistakes can be difficult.

If you receive an unwanted grade on a piece of written work, find out the reason. Again, think about the time and effort you expended on the paper and a realistic grade in relation to your performance. If you still feel dissatisfied, search for the reasons for your low grade. Start by reading the instructor's comments on the paper. If there are few or no comments, ask for an appointment so you can find out the reason or reasons for the low grade. You can also examine the paper yourself or have a friend read it and give you feedback. The important factor is to determine the problem or problems that caused the low grade. Was it poor organization? poor development of the paper? inappropriate content? inappropriate treatment of the content? writing quality? failure to follow instructions? some other problem? Remember, you can't correct the problem until you identify it.

You may complete four years of college without ever receiving a low grade on a paper or an exam. If so, great! If you do receive a poor grade (by your standards), however, try to handle it in such a way that you can learn from the experience. You should now allow a poor grade to devastate you, because then it is hard to recover and maintain a good mental attitude. Turn the negative experience into a positive one by learning from it.

Savvy is . . .

knowing how your instructors function: how they teach, how they grade, and what their expectations are. Some students call this "psyching out the prof." In high school, it was a game to find ways to distract teachers and lead them off on a tangent that could consume the entire class time. That can also be done in college, but you may still be held accountable for the material whether or not it is covered. Here, psyching out the prof means simply figuring out how he or she functions in relation to a number of items such as those listed here.

1. *Does the instructor use the same teaching method all the time?* Some instructors lecture almost all the time; others use techniques such as discussion, simulation, small groups, student reports, and the like. The teaching method could impact you in a number of ways. If you are a good auditory learner, then lectures may be your thing. If you enjoy active processing, however, lectures will not be your cup of tea. Although you probably can't have much influence on how an instructor teaches, you can work to accommodate different styles.

2. *Does the instructor expect you to participate in class discussions?* In smaller classes where discussion is feasible, some instructors want to involve students actively, which is an excellent teaching method. You

need to know how your instructor views the purpose of class discussion. Is it to change the pace of class activities or to develop the lesson? Does participation in class discussion contribute to your grade? If such items are not indicated in the syllabus, ask.

3. *Does the instructor provide clear expectations for students?* A syllabus should contain objectives or expectations that spell out what students are expected to know or what skills they should develop. If these expectations are clear, you should be able to guide your own learning to some extent. The stated expectations or objectives should indicate whether you are expected to know material from a factual viewpoint, an interpretative viewpoint, an analytical viewpoint, some other level of learning, or all of the above. The syllabus should also indicate the expectations and the criteria for evaluating written work.

4. *What is the instructor's overall evaluation policy?* What constitutes your grade? How are the various assignments, exams, and other activities valued? Some instructors base a grade only on the exams — perhaps a midterm and a final. Others, who give short quizzes and require papers of various types or other assignments, base the grade on more than just exams. It is important to know how the various pieces of work are valued in relation to the final grade. Not knowing the value of various graded work could cause you to spend an inordinate amount of time on a minor piece of work.

5. *What are the instructor's grading standards?* Most instructors assign a point value to each assignment and to the exams. You need to know how many or what percentage of the points are required for an A, B, C, and so on. By knowing such information, you can keep track of your progress and be aware when you have to study extra hard or put together an excellent paper.

6. *Does the instructor provide an opportunity for you to retake a test or rewrite a paper?* Some instructors are concerned with the competencies you develop through the class. Because they want you to acquire the knowledge and/or skills, they will give you a second chance. In such cases, you need to know the relationship of the two grades: Are they averaged, is only the second attempt counted, or is some other method used to determine the grade?

7. *Does the instructor return exams and written work quickly?* Feedback about your performance is helpful for improving future performance, and that feedback is of greatest value when you get it quickly. If an instructor waits too long to return papers or exams, part of your motivation for improving may disappear. Actually, there may be little you can do in this case except to ask the instructor to return work more promptly.

8. *What type of exams does the instructor give?* You should know early

in the term the type of exams an instructor gives because that knowledge can influence the way you prepare. Preparation for an exam does not begin two days before the exam; it begins when you attend the first lecture and read the first chapter in the book. You are likely to read or listen differently if you know exams are going to be essay rather than objective.

9. *Is the instructor friendly, understanding, and approachable?* Some university professors are, unfortunately, not too interested in spending time helping students with learning problems or analyzing an exam or paper. Although this is the exception rather than the rule, a few professors still feel their job is to share their knowledge only through lectures. These professors may not be amenable to listening to your concerns or problems or may not show any understanding after listening. If you run into this type of instructor, it may be difficult to gain the personal help you may need.

10. *How does the instructor function during class presentation?* Whatever teaching method the instructor uses, certain interactive characteristics or teaching behaviors can have an impact on the learner. The following series of questions may give you insight into this matter.
    a. Does the instructor seek student contributions and then recognize contributions and correct answers? This behavior indicates an instructor who is interested in including students actively, which is a good teaching technique.
    b. Does the instructor allow or even welcome questions during a lecture, or does he or she ask you to hold your questions until the end of the class? The instructor who allows questions when students need to ask them seems to be open to student involvement.
    c. Does the instructor phrase questions clearly or are they fuzzy or incomprehensible? Sometimes an instructor will purposely ask a fuzzy question to see if a student will seek clarification. In general, however, clear questions seem to suggest good preplanning.
    d. Does the instructor use good presentation techniques? These are specific behaviors associated with each teaching method. For example, when lecturing, an instructor should use examples, use illustrations, let you know where he or she is trying to take you, ask questions for clarification, use summary statements periodically, make eye contact, recognize when students tune out, use various methods to hold students' attention, and close the lecture with a general summary of the content for that day.
    e. Does the instructor give you tips or clues by the way he or she emphasizes important content? As indicated in a later chapter, the good listener will pick up on these clues if they are provided, but sometimes students miss those clues. For example, one professor, when lecturing on a topic the first class session, always tells students

that a question on that topic will appear on the final exam. Almost invariably a few students will miss the question, even though it is fairly straightforward, because they failed to note the instructor's specific statement that it would be on the test.

Obviously this list could go on and on, but it may not be productive to include additional items. The listed items are provided to help you gain a better understanding of your professors and how they function. The wise student will add additional items to the list. Now, how do you acquire this information about your instructors?

First, you must be a good observer of what goes on in your classes. Listen carefully to what your instructors say and assess the literal and figurative meaning of their statements. Notice their nonverbal behavior, such as empha- sized hand movements or intense facial expressions, because the nonverbal can reveal much to the astute observer. Further note their *task orientation*: Do they stay with the topic or wander off in various directions? Digressions can be both exciting and rewarding, but will you be held responsible for the content not covered during these rambles? Pay attention to any stated *procedure*, such as not interrupting to ask questions.

Second, try to determine what *policies* instructors have. Some professors believe it is the student's problem if he or she does not attend class. It is the student's money and the student's record, their thinking runs, so why bother to have a policy? Others have policies about absence and lateness to class. They feel that students should be in class on a regular basis because it improves their chances of succeeding; some also expect students to be on time because they don't like to be interrupted with people coming into class late.

It may be difficult to believe, but a few professors become irritated when students talk to each other, read nonrelated material during class, laugh, blow their noses, and so on. A generation ago, there was a professor who taught modern European history at a large Midwestern university. He was extremely knowledgeable and competent, an outstanding lecturer. If a student coughed during one of his classes, which usually contained 300 to 400 students, he would walk off the podium and hand the student a cough drop. Students who talked with each other during the lecture were asked to leave. No one com- plained, though, because he was such an excellent instructor.

Whatever your instructor's individual policies about class behavior may be, you should respect these policies even if you don't agree with them. If a professor does not want students coming to class late, you won't endear yourself to him or her by breaking that rule. In short, it's a good idea to follow policies set forth by instructors.

Third, ask other students about instructors. Students who have been around for several years will know about the idiosyncrasies of various instruc- tors and how these little quirks and traits will or will not affect the student. Experienced students are usually happy to talk about instructors; push them into giving you specific information, though, not general opinions. For example, if a student tells you that Professor X is tough, ask what it is that makes him or her tough. Some professors do not like students to attempt to talk with them after class. This may be an idiosyncrasy; but it may also reflect the fact that the professor has another class, appointment, or meeting and would rather talk with you during his or her office hours. Other students can give you information about such behaviors if you only ask.

Savvy is . . .

taking care of yourself, mentally and physically. Along with improving your ability to write, read, listen, remember, and take notes, also pay attention to the way you care for your own body; otherwise, all your good efforts may count for nothing. Sometimes we perform acts of omission and commission against our bodies. An *act of omission* is simply failing to do some thing we should do, such as eating properly. On the other hand, an *act of commission* is doing something to our bodies we should not do.

As a college student, you may be away from home for an extended time for the first time in your life, or, if not away from home, you may have a level of independence you previously did not have. You may now be expected to take charge of your life, which means that you make your own decisions and guide your own destiny. Taking charge of your life is part of the maturing process and can be exciting, but keep in mind that taking charge also includes mundane matters such as doing the laundry and buying toilet articles. Let's look closer at some of those factors related to taking care of yourself.

• • • • • • • • •

MAINTAINING GOOD NUTRITION

• • • • • • • • •

Your body needs certain vitamins and minerals in certain amounts to function properly. Usually, a balanced diet consisting of food from the basic food groups you learned in elementary school will provide you with enough of the right nutrients. If, however, you snack too much, eat on the run, eat too much fast food or too much sugar, you may not be getting enough of the essential nutrients. If you don't think you get enough nutrients, read a good book on nutrition and consider supplementing your food intake with a multiple vitamin. Eventually, you may reap the negative effects of poor nutrition.

• • • • • • • • •

GETTING PLENTY OF SLEEP

• • • • • • • • •

Individuals vary in their need for sleep, but there is probably a minimum needed for a high level of alertness. Most people cannot go day after day with less sleep than they need and still perform satisfactorily. Figure out what your sleep/wake cycle is and pay attention to what your body tells you.

• • • • • • • • • •

TAKING THE TIME TO RELAX

• • • • • • • • •

Sometimes we become so involved with study, work, and social life that we forget to take the time to relax. Build some time into your schedule for taking it easy. If you have only a short time for relaxation, enhance it by doing a few mental relaxation exercises or do deep breathing just before relaxing.

• • • • • • • • • •

GETTING PLENTY OF EXERCISE

• • • • • • • • •

Exercise or physical activity such as walking, handball, tennis, jogging, riding a bike, or whatever you enjoy helps relieve the tension that builds up from a busy schedule. Besides relieving tension, exercise helps you to maintain a healthy cardiovascular system.

• • • • • • • • • •

BEING REALISTIC WITH TIME COMMITMENTS

• • • • • • • • •

Don't overcommit your time. One of the best things you can learn to say is "No" to demands on your time when you already have enough to do. It is important to be involved in campus or off-campus activities, but these must be kept in perspective with your main mission, which is learning. Becoming too involved in nonacademic activities can lead to poor performance in the academic sphere. Poor performance, especially when you know you can do better, can lead to guilt feelings, which can be self-defeating and affect all aspects of your life. The thinner you spread yourself, the more vulnerable you are to failure.

Continued failure can also create feelings of inadequacy and lead to a lowered self-concept. It is easy to get so involved in nonacademic activities that the academic dimension of going to college becomes secondary. If you have the ability and skill to perform at a high level but fail to do so because of too much nonacademic involvement, your guilt feelings can become strong. Such feelings seem to be self-feeding and can affect all areas of your life. *Keep in mind that if you spread yourself too thin, you become vulnerable to failure*. It is important to recognize that you can't do everything you desire. Strive to do well what is feasible within your time constraints.

• • • • • • • • •

CONTROLLING YOUR ALCOHOLIC INTAKE

• • • • • • • • •

Individuals differ in their tolerance for alcohol and it is important that you discover yours if you consume alcoholic beverages. Then respect the limits your body provides. Failure to respect those natural limits can, as you already know, lead to serious problems. Short of serious problems, too much alcohol can impair the ability of your body to function as it was designed to. Alcohol destroys some of the nutrients you need for a healthy body. It also impairs judgment, distorts perception, interferes with your ability to concentrate, your desire to work, and the nature of your interpersonal relations. Although the actual negative feelings associated with too much alcohol soon leave, the negative influence on physical and mental functions lingers. The morning after can have a disastrous effect on your ability to concentrate.

• • • • • • • • •

UNDERSTANDING THE NEGATIVE EFFECTS OF CHEMICAL SUBSTANCES

• • • • • • • • •

Drugs alter your mood, sensation, muscle coordination, and thinking. Many drugs have medical usefulness, but some have side effects that are not at all medically useful. Because drugs affect your thinking, they obviously affect your ability to be an effective student. Let us examine some of these drugs and their specific effects (Brown, 1983).

Sedatives suppress or inhibit many functions of the brain. Sedatives include alcohol and barbiturates, which are general brain depressants and which interfere with wakefulness, judgment, inhibitions, mood, and muscle coordination.

Stimulants include amphetamines and cocaine, which excite the brain cells by facilitating signals between neurons. These substances do, in fact, reduce fatigue, enhance mood, increase alertness and motor skills. What seems to be a positive, however, hides a much larger negative: People take such drugs for many reasons, one of which is to think more clearly. But such drugs actually increase distractibility; thus, thinking becomes more confused and the ability to concentrate lost.

Opiates such as morphine reduce pain, but they are also habit forming. *Hallucinogenics* such as LSD, mescaline, and PCP cause distortion of sounds, images, tastes, and smells as well as other sensations. Hallucinogens distract the ability of neurons to transmit messages properly because, for some reason, the neurons think the drugs themselves are transmitters. Therefore the neurons, the message carriers in the brain, become confused and may induce abnormal behavior. *Marijuana*, the drug that many feel is the safest, can cause disaster, because it clearly reduces intellectual performance, interferes with short-term memory and time perception, and impairs psychomotor skills.

It is safe to say that the uses and abuses of chemical substances represent one of the major social and economic problems today. Most people probably begin using drugs to have fun or because of pressure from friends. The false sense of well-being that develops may cause additional use. Continued use leads to addiction and the individual loses a great deal of control over his/her life. It is in just this loss of self-control that academic disaster lies. The inability to think clearly, concentrate effectively, and make sound judgments add up to a loss of personal control that makes it very difficult to be an effective student.

Other than loss of life or physical disability, perhaps the most negative factor in substance abuse is the destruction of self-concept. It is likely that those who use drugs, who abuse their bodies and minds, do not think much of themselves. The use of drugs represents one way of hiding from self, from life and the challenges and demands faced each day. Drugs do not represent a cure for the problems of life — only a place to hide. There are many real sources of help available for the person who wants to face life head on rather than run and hide. Certainly the student who uses and/or abuses chemical substances greatly reduces his/her chances of being a successful student and a successful person.

If you feel that drugs, alcohol, guilt, depression, anxiety, or any one of a number of other conditions is negatively affecting your ability to function properly, act quickly. Share your situation with someone who is a good listener — someone who may be able to help you understand the situation better. Professional counselors are available on campus or at social service agencies in the community. The important thing is to know when you need help and seek it.

Review

It is important to develop goal-directed behavior during your college life. Goal-directed behavior will help you succeed not only in college but also in life. If you haven't already carefully examined your motivation, take the time to consider seriously why you are going to college. Remember, if you are not in college because you really want to be there, achieving success will be hard. Your motivation and drive to succeed can overcome many obstacles, including inadequate or poor academic background.

You can increase your chances of succeeding by developing a high level of awareness about the services available to you on campus. Besides the basic service offices, you must locate the library and the computer center and learn how to make full use of both these resources.

Dealing effectively with conflict and disappointment will also facilitate your success. Worrying about your problems rather than solving them can have a negative effect on your performance and can cause you undue stress.

Paying attention to instructors and their individual teaching styles is a common practice among successful college students, who make sure they know each instructor's expectations and requirements. They study the way their instructors teach, how they grade, their policies about lateness, attendance, late papers, and the like. In short, it can be very helpful to you to know as much about the way your instructor functions as you can.

Taking care of your mental and physical needs properly in terms of food, sleep, exercise, and relaxation can improve your ability to function properly. Avoiding substances that abuse your mental and physical functions helps ensure that you will deliver your best possible performance.

Review Questions

1. What, in your opinion, are three or four good reasons for attending college? Why do you feel they are good reasons? Is your motivation appropriate?

2. Why are scores on intelligence tests overrated in terms of success in college?

3. How is your background appropriate to success in college?

4. What are the various support services available to you on campus? How can each help you?

5. How does functional conflict differ from dysfunctional conflict? Is your primary current conflict primarily functional or dysfunctional?

6. What are the four types of conflict?

7. What method or methods do you use to manage your conflict? Do these methods generally work for you? If not what can you do?

8. What are some of the ways you can learn how your professor functions?

9. How can knowledge about your instructor enhance your success in college?

10. How can you deal with disappointments and setbacks in a positive way?

11. What do you do to care for your body properly?

12. How do drugs and alcohol interfere with learning?

References

Brown, Roger. "How Do Drugs Affect The Brain?" *Science Challenge* (November 1983): pp. 11–12. (The section on drugs was adapted from Brown's article.)

Cattell, Raymond B. *Abilities: Their Structure, Growth, and Action.* Boston, Mass.: Houghton Mifflin, 1971, p. 9.

Charlesworth, William R. "Human Intelligence as Adaptation: An Ethological Approach." In Lauren B. Resnick, ed., *The Nature of Intelligence.* Hillsdale, N.J.: Lawrence Erlbaum Associates, 1976, pp. 148–149.

Frey, Diane E. "Understanding and Managing Conflict." In S. Eisenberg, and L. Patterson, eds., *Helping Clients with Special Concerns.* New York: Rand McNally, 1979.

Resnick, Lauren B. and Robert Glaser. "Problem Solving and Intelligence." In Lauren B. Resnick, ed., *The Nature of Intelligence.* Hillsdale, N.J.: Lawrence Erlbaum Associates, 1976, p. 205.

Thomas, Kenneth and Ralph Kilmann. *Conflict Mode Instrument.* Xicom, Inc., n.d. (Conflict management styles adapted from author's descriptions.)

Voss, James F. "The Nature of 'The Nature of Intelligence.'" In Lauren B. Resnick, ed., *The Nature of Intelligence.* Hillsdale, N.J.: Lawrence Erlbaum Associates, 1976, p. 309.

UNDERSTANDING LEARNING AS A KEY TO SUCCESS

The process of learning may be one of the most heavily studied human activities since modern research began. During the last hundred years, a wide range of learning theories and their offshoots have emerged; research findings have been reported in books and journals and applied in countless classrooms. From these studies we have discovered much about the way human beings intake, process, remember, and access information. We know more about ways to study, retain, motivate, and forget than ever before. It is likely, however, that many college students are not consciously aware of much of the rich harvest of information on learning.

This chapter will attempt to bridge that gap by providing you with some basic information on the process of learning. If you come to understand your own learning process better, you will be able to assess how well it works for you and develop new learning strategies if necessary. The goals of this chapter are:

1. To help you understand more about the mental activity we call *learning*
2. To help you learn more about theories of learning
3. To help you develop effective learning strategies
4. To help you understand learning styles and preferences
5. To help you understand the role of the brain in learning

WHAT IS LEARNING?

Though they often overlap, the definitions of learning are numerous. Each theorist seems to have his or her own way of describing the process, but a common thread suggests that learning represents a *change in behavior. Behavior* here refers to the way an individual functions at the level of either thinking or action. Suppose you heard, for example, that people who eat large amounts of a certain food are more likely to develop cancer of the colon later in life than those who don't. If, after eating that food in large amounts, you then either reduce the amount or stop eating it altogether, you have changed your behavior. If you answer a question on an exam correctly because you reviewed the relevant material the night before, you also experienced a change in behavior. Is learning always accompanied by a change in behavior? That is a philosophical question, not an empirical one that can be answered in a scientific experiment. A definition of learning that includes the capability of a change in behavior, however, would probably be acceptable to most researchers.

THEORIES OF LEARNING

As indicated earlier, a number of learning theories have been developed over the past century. These theories are attempts to explain learning through systematically developed principles or sets of principles. The whole purpose of developing theories about learning, of course, is to try to predict when it will occur. Knowledge of how learning works makes it possible to arrange conditions to facilitate the process. Certainly this is true up to a point, but human beings, having their idiosyncrasies, do not always follow the pattern or process predicted, nor do they always respond to prearranged conditions. Thus, though learning theory provides a framework for studying how people learn, it may not predict or explain the learning process for any given individual.

There are three major groups or families of learning theories. Each theory within these three groups differs slightly from the others, but there are common elements; thus, for our purposes, some general statements about the groups of theories can be made here.

1. *Mental discipline theories* are characterized by:
   a. Training of students' minds. Some subjects such as geometry and Latin are considered good subjects to discipline or train one's mind.
   b. Drill, memorization, retention and frequent testing.
   c. Control of students' behavior by punishment or threats of punishment to improve attention and study. According to this theory, well-behaved students who are drilled and tested frequently in the appropriate subjects will learn. This was certainly the most common approach to learning well into the twentieth century.

2. *Stimulus response* or *behavioral theories* characterized by:
   a. Associations or connections between stimuli and responses.
   b. Use of rewards.
   c. Repetition or practice to strengthen the bonds between stimulus and response.
   d. Teachers' control over learning conditions and procedures.

   In summary, if the correct response is associated with a certain stimulus, is repeated frequently and rewarded properly, learning occurs.

3. *Cognitive field* or *Gestalt theories* are characterized by these precepts:
   a. The learner has a clear purpose in the learning activities.
   b. The learner interacts with and understands people.
   c. The process of learning is as important as the outcomes.
   d. The learner's perception of reality is important.
   e. The learner gains understanding of self and the surrounding environment.

f. The learner gains new insights into the environment.

Here the learning process is less teacher directed than in stimulus response theories. Learning is based on goals and the understanding of self and the environment.

These learning theories have inspired a great deal of research on learning. From that research a number of ideas or principles have emerged that should be helpful to you personally in guiding your own learning. The following is a list of statements based on research on learning. Read this list carefully and decide if you agree or disagree with the items in terms of your experience. Write *A* or *D* on the line provided.

_____ 1. Learned responses that are not used over a period of time will not be easily accessible.

_____ 2. When a response or behavior is followed by a reward or a personally satisfying experience, that response or behavior is more likely to occur again.

_____ 3. The ease of learning the material affects the amount of effort expended.

_____ 4. Similar materials are retained longest if they are learned at separated periods of time.

_____ 5. Reading followed by recitation will lead to better retention than silent reading by itself.

_____ 6. Study followed by sleep often facilitates recall because fewer activities have occurred in the interval.

_____ 7. Learning is generally more efficient if study is interspersed with periods of rest, relaxation, or self-recitation (recalling aloud, recalling silently, visualizing, etc.).

_____ 8. Learners remember new information that confirms previous ideas or knowledge.

_____ 9. Recall immediately after learning reduces the amount the learner will forget.

_____ 10. Learners who have faith in themselves are more likely to succeed than learners who don't.

_____ 11. Practice and repetition are more valuable if feedback on the success of these efforts is provided.

_____ 12. Fresh or novel experiences can enhance success in learning.

_____ 13. Too much frustration can interfere with the motivation to pursue a goal, and thus with learning.

_____ 14. Active participation in the learning process can increase motivation.

_____ 15. Learning is easier if the knowledge is perceived as useful.

How does your experience as a learner relate to these statements about learning? Because learning is an individual matter, not all the items will apply to everyone. Can you improve your learning by making use of some of these principles? Think about the items on this list over which you have control and try to use those principles when you read and study.

LEARNING STYLES OR PREFERENCES

Most people have clear preferences in ways of learning as in other areas of their everyday lives. In fact, learning and daily life are closely intertwined. A *learning style* is simply a way of learning you know and practice. A *learning preference* is the particular learning style or styles an individual inclines toward. What does it mean to have a learning preference? Some people prefer visual learning; that is, they would rather learn using their eyes. Others, however, prefer to learn by hearing or speaking. Still others find tactile learning the easiest. Usually a person can potentially make use of a number of learning styles even though he or she may naturally prefer one style over the others. The interesting fact about learning styles is that even though individuals usually are able to use more than one style, they often don't; they simply rely on their old standby. A major goal of this section will be to help you identify your style or styles of learning.

As a way of getting a handle on styles and preferences, think about people you know well. How differently do you function from others in your circle? You like math, the other person likes art. You like to plan your life carefully, the other person is spontaneous and freewheeling. You like listening to lectures, the other person prefers to read the text. Certainly these are different styles of functioning. Except in specific situations, though, it is impossible to say whether one style is better than another. For example, one of your professors requires that all assignments be turned in on time. You, however, tend to do assignments at the last minute and are sometimes late turning them in. Will this behavior be a detriment to you?

Why are we all different? Some say heredity, others say environment, and still others say it is a combination of both. The last of these is probably the most accurate — certainly the safest — statement. Individual differences are what make each of us unique and also provide the reasons that one theory of learning, one way of teaching, or one way of doing things is not universally applicable. Some teachers are aware of learning differences and work to accommodate them, but many are not; it is unusual to find college teachers who try to accommodate the different learning styles of their students. Therefore, you need to understand your learning styles and preferences in order to adapt them to a given learning situation and thereby gain a measure of control.

In the last fifty years, large amounts of time, energy, and money have gone into studying, documenting and recording individual differences in styles of learning and living. The numerous personality and preference instruments now available represent some of that research. The overall goal of creating and using such instruments is to help individuals understand the way they function. Such instruments are also used in employment counseling, marriage counseling, and identifying learning problems.

Hemispheric Specialization

One of the significant pieces of research related to our understanding of the human brain was conducted by Dr. Roger Sperry and his associates at the California Institute of Technology during the 1950s and 1960s. This research related to the *corpus callosum* in the brain, a band of about 200 million nerve fibers that carry messages between the two hemispheres (right and left) of the brain. The corpus callosum was thought to play a role in the severity of epileptic seizures. If the seizure started in one hemisphere of the brain, it seemed to be intensified in the other hemisphere; therefore, it was believed that as the seizure traveled through the corpus callosum it became stronger in the other side. After experiments with animals, in 1961 Sperry and his associates succeeded in severing the corpus callosum in a human brain (Restak, 1979). They actually cut the fibers connecting the corpus callosum to each hemisphere of the brain in the hope that the epileptic seizure would be less severe. The surgery did, in fact, reduce the severity of the seizures but virtually created two persons, which is the reason for referring to individuals having had such surgery as split-brain patients. Because the right and left hemispheres could no longer communicate with each other, this fact made it possible for researchers to pinpoint the specific mental functions performed in each hemisphere of the brain.

To grasp this effect fully, you must understand the paths of the visual fields. The *right visual field*—what you see when you look to the right— feeds into the left hemisphere, and the *left visual field* feeds into the right hemisphere. Because messages do not travel between hemispheres in split-brain patients, the information stays in the side of the brain where it was originally received. By displaying common objects that could only be seen by one of the visual fields, researchers could determine the functions of each hemisphere. For example a spoon, balloon, pencil, and cup might be held up in such a way that they were only visible in the right visual field. When the patient was then asked to name the objects or reach out with the right hand and pick up the spoon, the request was performed. This was because the left hemisphere in most people contains the language centers—the centers that can name or recognize an object. (The left hemisphere is verbal.) If, however, the objects were exposed to the left visual field and the person was asked to pick up the spoon with his left hand, the request could not be performed because the right hemisphere is primarily visual and nonverbal. When asked to draw an object that was seen, however, the request could be met.

The research with split brain patients documented that the two hemispheres do perform different mental functions. In persons whose corpus callosum is intact, however, these differences are readily not apparent because communication between the two hemispheres remains intact. Nonetheless, many individuals do have clear preferences in the way they think and function: Some incline toward the right hemispheric functions; others toward the left hemispheric functions. Still others have no strong preferences and are comfortable with the functions of either hemisphere. It is important to remember that the word *preference* does not necessarily mean competence or strength. Equally, lack of a preference for left or right does not necessarily mean incompetence or weakness. It is, however, likely that an individual will be more effective in one area than in the other.

People in certain occupations seem to use one hemisphere more than the other. For example, accountants, computer specialists, administrators, research scientists, many medical doctors, and mathematicians seem to draw heavily on the left hemispheric functions. On the other hand, elementary teachers, many nurses, psychiatrists, social workers, ministers, artists, and musicians are likely to draw heavily on the right hemispheric functions. Architects, company presidents, entrepreneurs, politicians, behavioral researchers, secondary teachers, and technical writers are likely to draw on the functions of both hemispheres.

Now, given this background, where do you stand? Do you prefer the left hemispheric functions, the right hemispheric functions, or are you without a preference? If you have a preference, is it weak, medium, or strong? Complete the following preference inventory.

Directions.   Choose which item below — a, b, or c — you prefer. It may be difficult to make choices in some cases, but choose the one you think is most descriptive. Mark only one — a, b, or c — for each numbered item. To learn what your responses mean, see the answer key at the end of this chapter.

1. I prefer
   _____ a. to learn auditorially.
   _____ b. to learn visually.
   _____ c. both ways equally.

2. I prefer
   _____ a. work that is conceptual.
   _____ b. work that is technical.
   _____ c. both kinds equally.

3. I usually prefer
   _____ a. essay tests.
   _____ b. multiple choice, true/false tests.
   _____ c. both equally.

4. When reading or listening, I usually try
   _____ a. to focus on the main ideas.
   _____ b. to focus on the facts and details.
   _____ c. to focus on both facts and main ideas.

5. When I have a number of tasks to do, I usually prefer
   _____ a. to organize those in sequence.
   _____ b. to perform the tasks randomly.
   _____ c. to use both ways of functioning.

6. I enjoy
   _____ a. guessing at possible solutions to problems.
   _____ b. figuring out solutions analytically.
   _____ c. both ways equally.

7. I
   _____ a. usually do not get lost finding my way around.
   _____ b. sometimes get lost.
   _____ c. frequently get lost.

8. I tend to
   _____ a. respond to emotion.
   _____ b. respond to realism.
   _____ c. respond to both equally.

9. I prefer to learn material that is
   _____ a. primarily verbal.
   _____ b. primarily spatial.
   _____ c. both equally.

10. In terms of time management, I
    _____ a. usually organize my time carefully.
    _____ b. sometimes organize my time carefully.
    _____ c. rarely organize my time carefully.

11. I like to
    _____ a. solve problems with logic.
    _____ b. solve problems in terms of how I feel about them.
    _____ c. use both approaches.

12. When I am with another person, I usually
    _____ a. observe their body language more than I listen to what is said.
    _____ b. listen and observe body language.
    _____ c. listen carefully for the words used more than I observe body
             language.

13. I like to
    _____ a. identify the facts that make up an idea.

_____ b. put facts together to form an idea.

_____ c. use both approaches.

14. I like to

_____ a. study material that I can apply right away.

_____ b. study material that may be of value someday.

_____ c. study both kinds equally.

15. I prefer to learn

_____ a. by sitting and listening to what someone says.

_____ b. by being actively involved in the learning process.

_____ c. both ways equally.

16. I prefer games

_____ a. of logic.

_____ b. that involve risks.

_____ c. both types equally.

17. I prefer

_____ a. to think imaginatively.

_____ b. to think realistically.

_____ c. both ways equally.

18. I prefer

_____ a. to complete one task before beginning another.

_____ b. to begin a second or third task before completing the first.

_____ c. both equally.

19. I prefer

_____ a. classes where facts are emphasized.

_____ b. classes where creativity is emphasized.

_____ c. both equally.

20. I prefer

_____ a. an organized lifestyle.

_____ b. sometimes organized and sometimes flexible.

_____ c. a flexible lifestyle.

21. I like

_____ a. to try out new things or ideas.

_____ b. to do what I know works.

_____ c. both equally well.

22. When taking notes, I

_____ a. usually try to make an outline.

_____ b. usually make summary statements.

_____ c. use both methods.

23. I usually

_____ a. remember faces well.

_____ b. remember names well.

_____ c. remember both equally well.

24. I enjoy
    _____ a. thinking about things real.
    _____ b. thinking about what could be.
    _____ c. both equally.

25. I enjoy
    _____ a. reading things that are fantasy based.
    _____ b. reading things that are technical.
    _____ c. reading either type.

26. I prefer
    _____ a. verbal explanations.
    _____ b. explanations with examples or visual aids.
    _____ c. both equally.

27. I prefer
    _____ a. to plan carefully.
    _____ b. to take things as they come.
    _____ c. to plan sometimes.

28. I
    _____ a. usually keep my work area neat.
    _____ b. usually have a disorganized work area.
    _____ c. sometimes have a neat work area.

29. I prefer
    _____ a. rational discussions.
    _____ b. intuitive discussions.
    _____ c. both equally.

30. I prefer
    _____ a. expressing myself with words.
    _____ b. expressing myself with designs or pictures.
    _____ c. both equally.

Though this inventory has not been scientifically validated, it should provide you with information about your hemispheric preferences. If you scored about 15 on one of the three (left, right, or whole), that score would seem to be a fairly clear preference. If your scores are fairly evenly distributed, you probably prefer using both hemispheres equally. To help you understand some of the items, the following is a list of words that generally describe the functions of each hemisphere (Herrmann, 1985).

LEFT	RIGHT
1. Detailed	1. Intuitive
2. Sequential	2. Symbolic
3. Conservative	3. Spiritual
4 Logical	4 Emotional
5. Mathematical	5. Spatial

6. Rational
7. Analytical
8. Factual
9. Quantitative
10. Critical
11. Technical
12. Organized

6. Simultaneous
7. Holistic
8. Creative
9. Artistic
10. Synthesized
11. Conceptual
12. Random

How do these descriptions relate to your strengths or preferences? Which of these terms are descriptive of courses whose subject matter or presentation you like or don't like? How do these preferences relate to your performance?

Now what does all this mean for you as a college student? You will encounter professors who structure their classes in such a way that the lectures, assignments, and tests are geared to the right or left hemispheric specialization. If you happen to prefer the same specialization, the class may be easier for you. If, on the other hand, you prefer the opposite specialization, you will have to learn to accommodate a different type of thinking. The same is true of subject matter. Some subjects such as math, science, and accounting are highly logical, linear, orderly, sequential, or analytical. If your preferences are holistic, intuitive, spatial, creative, and emotional rather than the foregoing, you may have to develop some new preferences. You may, of course, have both sets of preferences. Many of us can use or learn to use the less preferred hemisphere simply by thinking about the need to use it. Others may need to work harder to use the less preferred side effectively. Becoming involved in activities that require you to use the less preferred hemisphere could be helpful in gaining increased flexibility.

If you prefer the right hemisphere thinking and want to learn to use the left, try some of the following suggestions (Herrmann, 1985):

1. Keep careful records of your favorite baseball or football team.
2. Develop a personal budget and follow it.
3. Perform an activity that requires you to follow careful directions.
4. Play games of logic.
5. Organize your room, pictures, or phonograph records.
6. Outline material from a textbook.
7. Follow the progress of a few stocks even if you can't afford to buy them; calculate their growth or decline.
8. Build models.
9. Learn to use a computer.
10. Play games with strict, complicated rules.

If you strongly prefer left hemisphere thinking and want to learn to draw upon the right more, try some of the following activities (Herrmann, 1985):

1. Read poetry, particularly emotional or inspirational poetry.
2. Daydream, imagine yourself doing something different.
3. Play the music you like.
4. Invent something.
5. Watch people.
6. Write something imaginative.
7. Do aerobic dancing.
8. Learn photography.
9. Do bird watching.
10. Do church or volunteer work.

Psychological Types

The scheme described here is based on the work of Carl Gustav Jung, a Swiss psychoanalyst, earlier in this century. Jung (1923) postulated that people function in terms of three psychological types. These types are polarities, that is, linear dimensions with opposite attributes at each end of the scale. Further, he suggested that our attitudes toward the inner/outer world fall somewhere on the scale between two opposite attributes, *extraversion* and *introversion*. The other two dimensions are called *functions* and relate to the way we perceive or intake information and to the way we process or judge that information. The first of these dimensions, *perception*, has two attributes called *sensing* and *intuition* at opposite ends. The second dimension has two attributes called *thinking* and *feeling* at opposite ends. A graphic of Jung's opposing attributes might look like this:

EXTRAVERSION ——————— INTROVERSION
SENSING ——————— INTUITION
THINKING ——————— FEELING

Not long after Jung's *Psychological Types* was published, Katharine Briggs began similar work in the United States. Briggs, joined by her daughter Isabel Briggs (later Myers), added a dimension to Jung's psychological types. The fourth, like the first, is an attitude dimension, but is often referred to as a lifestyle dimension. Its categories are judging and perception and could be shown in the same way as Jung's polarities.

JUDGING ——————— PERCEPTIVE

Briggs and Myers went further than Jung in attempting to make the theory practical by developing an instrument (1943) to measure individuals' preferences on each of the dimensions. The instrument, called the *Myers-Briggs Type Indicator*, yields scores on the four dimensions indicated here. Before looking at what you could learn from this indicator, a word of caution. As with the hemispheric specialization, preference does not necessarily indicate competence, nor does lack of preference indicate incompetence. Most of us function in the way we prefer to function until we meet a situation where we need to react differently. How flexible we are in those situations, where we must step outside our accustomed mode of operation, has much to do with success or failure. The purpose in presenting the following material is to help you become aware of your own preferred mode of function and to understand that others may function differently.

The Dimensions.   The four dimensions are:

1. *Extraversion* or *introversion:* how individuals relate to the inner/outer world.
2. *Sensing* or *intuition:* how individuals take in information.
3. *Thinking* or *feeling:* how individuals process or think or use that information in decision making.
4. *Judging* and *perception:* how individuals approach life or a lifestyle dimension.

A brief description of the dimensions follows. As you read, try to determine which characteristics in each column fit you, but also think about how you can make use of the other end of the dimension. Check the characteristic that describes you best.

1. The inner/outer world dimension is revealed through *extraversion* or *introversion*, which have the following characteristics.

Extraversion

Extraverted types tend to be characterized by:

_____ a. A desire to deal with people and things.

_____ b. Doing things, being action oriented.

_____ c. Having many acquaintances.

Introversion

Introverted types tend to be characterized by:

_____ a. A strong interest in ideas, concepts.

_____ b. Thinking about things, ideas.

_____ c. Having a few close friends.

_____	d.	Receiving stimulation from outward sources.	_____	d. Receiving stimulation from inner sources.
_____	e.	Preferring uncomplicated situations.	_____	e. An acceptance of complicated or complex situations.
_____	f.	A liking for large parties or gatherings.	_____	f. A liking for small parties or gatherings.
_____	g.	A concern for what others think.	_____	g. Inner reinforcement.
_____	h.	Acting quickly.	_____	h. Being slow to act.
_____	i.	Preferring short-term tasks.	_____	i. Liking long-range tasks.
_____	j.	Discussion and analysis with others.	_____	j. Discussion and analysis within oneself.

As you can see from these lists, extraverts and introverts seem to behave differently. Tune into the following conversations:

MARY: Joan, are you going to the party tonight?

JOAN: No, I really don't care for those big bashes.

MARY: Oh, you should go—you'll meet so many new people.

JOAN: I really prefer smaller parties of six to ten people. I think I'll stay home and study for my chemistry test.

Which of these two prefers extraversion? Obviously Mary has a preference for extraversion. Joan is uncomfortable in a situation where she does not know people and probably doesn't care to meet people in that type of situation. This does not mean that Joan is antisocial, just that she is more comfortable where she knows people.

2. The perception or finding-out dimension is shown through *sensing* or *intuition*, which have the following characteristics.

Sensing

Sensing types tend to be characterized by:

_____ a. A focus on the here and now.

_____ b. Dealing with practical things.

_____ c. Dealing with facts.

_____ d. Dealing with the concrete.

_____ e. Taking a step-by-step approach.

_____ f. Dealing with routine matters.

_____ g. A literal interpretation of things.

_____ h. Liking to use things learned.

_____ i. Not usually making errors about facts.

_____ j. Working steadily.

Intuition

Intuition types tend to be characterized by:

_____ a. A focus on the future.

_____ b. Dealing with imaginative things.

_____ c. An interest in how facts connect.

_____ d. Dealing with the abstract.

_____ e. Taking a look at the big picture.

_____ f. Dealing with unknown things.

_____ g. A figurative interpretation of things.

_____ h. Liking to learn to accumulate knowledge.

_____ i. Frequently make errors with facts.

_____ j. Working in spurts as moods strike them.

As you can see, there are distinct differences in the approaches taken toward finding out, both in method and content. For example:

PROFESSOR: Hi Kevin. How are things?

KEVIN: Okay. I just finished class.

PROFESSOR: Oh! What class is that?

KEVIN: Nothingness.

PROFESSOR: What?

KEVIN: Philosophy.

Kevin plans to major in marketing and apparently sees no relevance in, or application of, the subject of philosophy to his intended major. So it often is with sensors, because many have difficulty embracing material for which there is no immediate application. Intuitors, however, relish material that allows them to freewheel or think independently—to dream. Obviously, the two types view learning and its purpose differently and, in general, the kind of subjects they prefer. Intuitors often prefer those subjects where definite, correct answers are not very important, whereas sensors tend to prefer those subjects where definite correct answers are important. In which of these ways do you characteristically function?

3. The decision-making dimension includes *thinking* and *feeling*, which have the following characteristics.

Thinking

Thinking types tend to be characterized by:

———— a. Approaching problems logically.

———— b. Decision making based on facts.

———— c. A preference for responding to thoughts.

———— d. Objectively looking at matters.

———— e. A need to be treated fairly.

———— f. Able to deal with unpleasant things.

Feeling

Feeling types tend to be characterized by:

———— a. Approaching problems with feelings.

———— b. Decision making based on what matters to them.

———— c. A preference for responding to feelings.

———— d. Subjectively looking at matters.

———— e. A need for understanding and praise.

———— f. Not liking to deal with unpleasant things.

_____	g. A reluctance to show emotion.	_____	g. An awareness of emotion in themselves and others.
_____	h. Critical of things and people.	_____	h. Accepting of people.
_____	i. Viewing situations impersonally.	_____	i. Counseling people in a situation.
_____	j. Tough minded.	_____	j. Sympathetic or empathetic.

The following conversation should highlight some differences between *thinkers* and *feelers*.

WIFE: Honey, I'd like a Mercedes.

HUSBAND: My dear, a Mercedes costs about $40,000. How would we pay for it?

WIFE: I don't know, I just want one.

HUSBAND: Let's sit down and put the pencil to the problem and see what the numbers show.

The wife is used here as the feeler simply because about 60 percent of females prefer feeling over thinking. Again, notice the differences in functioning between the two types of decision makers. Do you veer more to the left column or the right column? Actually, you need both sets of behaviors or methods of functioning to survive. Certain decisions need to be made with the thinking function; others are better made with the feeling function. Many decisions should include both approaches to take into account different aspects of the decision. What you need to consider is whether or not you seem to be locked exclusively into one approach. You will probably be a more effective student if you can select and use the appropriate function, thinking or feeling, in a given situation. For example, use feeling on your spouse or friend and thinking on your carburetor.

   4. The lifestyle dimension includes *judging* and *perception*, which have the following characteristics.

Judgment

Judging types tend to be characterized by:

_____   a. Liking to plan.

Perception

Perceptive types tend to be characterized by:

_____   a. Liking to be spontaneous.

_____	b. Following a plan.	_____	b. Adapting to situations.
_____	c. Liking to settle things.	_____	c. Liking to keep issues open.
_____	d. Preferring a neat, orderly environment.	_____	d. Able to tolerate a disorderly environment.
_____	e. Deciding things quickly.	_____	e. Having some difficulty making decisions.
_____	f. Wanting to organize a job before beginning it.	_____	f. Starting a job and organizing as they proceed.
_____	g. Liking to schedule events of the day.	_____	g. Not liking to be tied down by a schedule.
_____	h. Having control over one's life.	_____	h. Being swept along by others.
_____	i. Meeting deadlines.	_____	i. Frequently being late.
_____	j. Liking to finish tasks.	_____	j. Working on various tasks at the same time.

The following conversation between a mother and father on a family motoring vacation illustrates one striking difference between judging and perceptive types.

DAD: Why don't we take a side trip over to see the Indian Mounds? It's only a hundred miles.

MOM: You know that's not on our itinerary.

DAD: I know and you won't depart from your plan. You wouldn't even go five miles out of your way to see that antique shop.

MOM: We have to stick with our plan or we won't get to L.A. in time.

Notice the difference in the thinking of the mother, the *judger*, and the father, the *perceptive type*. The judging type, for example, also tends to start working on a project such as a term paper when it is assigned, whereas the perceptive type tends to put the task off as long as possible. Judgers usually have their work in on time and they tend to be on time for meetings, classes, and so on. The perceptive types, on the other hand, more easily distracted by events around them, are much more likely to drift into some other activity than reading, writing a paper, or studying for an exam. Again, which type comes closer to describing you? If you can embrace both types appropriately, you are more likely to be a more effective student.

Now count your check marks in each column for each dimension. Which side, left or right do you favor? Did you have trouble deciding? Which characteristics are more descriptive of you? Sometimes individuals do not know their own preferences well and have a hard time making choices. Others find choices difficult because they can function equally at both ends of a dimension.

The point of this section was to help you understand that people learn and function in strikingly different ways. *You must not assume that professors are going to teach in a way that accommodates your preferred learning style or personal manner of functioning.* If you prefer to learn alone but the professor uses small groups, learn to adapt to that organization. If the professor sets the due date for a term paper the Monday after you are out of town for four days and you tend to do things at the last minute, you must concentrate on learning to plan better. If you prefer reading as your primary mode of learning but the professor bases exams largely on lecture, you must concentrate on learning to be a better listener.

The list of examples could go on and on, but you probably can think of many of your own. Do this. Think about how you prefer to learn and function. Then think about the nature of content of each course and the way each professor functions. Now ask yourself the following questions:

1. Do I think in the same way that the subject matter is organized? If I don't, how can I learn to think in the appropriate way?

2. Does the instructor function in a way that favors my preferred style? If not, what can I do to overcome the difference?

3. How do my learning and lifestyle preferences enhance or hinder my success in college?

4. If they hinder, can I, am I willing to make adjustments?

Review

Your understanding of how people learn — and, in particular, how *you* learn — can be an important key to your success in college. Three somewhat different learning theories have laid the foundation of much of modern research on learning. Some recent research related to learning has focused on learning styles that represent characteristic ways of functioning. It is important that you understand your own learning style or styles because this self-awareness will help you adapt successfully to the wide variety of learning situations you will encounter in college.

If the material in this chapter was not enough to give you adequate understanding of how you learn or brain hemispherity, you can investigate further.

1. Read from some of the references cited at the end of this chapter.

2. Find a professor on your campus who does research on learning styles or teaches learning styles and interview him or her. (Usually these professors will be found in the School of Education.)

3. Find someone on campus who can give you the *Myers-Briggs Type Indicator* or a good brain dominance instrument, such as the *Herrmann Participant Survey Form*. Few people are certified to give the Herrmann test, but there may be one on your campus. Usually a number of persons will be qualified to give the Myers-Briggs or another instrument that will help you understand your learning style. Check with the testing center on your campus or with the teacher education faculty.

Answer Key for Preference Inventory
R = right brain, L = left brain, W = whole brain

1. a–L, b–R, c–W	16. a–L, b–R, c–W
2. a–R, b–L, c–W	17. a–R, b–L, c–W
3. a–R, b–L, c–W	18. a–L, b–R, c–W
4. a–R, b–L, c–W	19. a–L, b–R, c–W
5. a–L, b–R, c–W	20. a–L, b–W, c–R
6. a–R, b–L, c–W	21. a–R, b–L, c–W
7. a–L, b–W, c–R	22. a–L, b–R, c–W
8. a–R, b–L, c–W	23. a–R, b–L, c–W
9. a–L, b–R, c–W	24. a–L, b–R, c–W
10. a–L, b–W, c–R	25. a–R, b–L, c–W
11. a–L, b–R, c–W	26. a–L, b–R, c–W
12. a–R, b–W, c–L	27. a–L, b–R, c–W
13. a–L, b–R, c–W	28. a–L, b–R, c–W
14. a–L, b–R, c–W	29. a–L, b–R, c–W
15. a–L, b–R, c–W	30. a–L, b–R, c–W

Review Questions

1. How do you define learning?

2. What are the major differences in the three basic learning theories? Which theory best describes the way you learn?

3. Do you have a preference in brain hemispherity? If so, is it a strong preference? Should you consider learning to function with your less preferred hemisphere?

4. Did the information related to the *Myers-Briggs Type Indicator* help you to understand how you function? If not, what could you do to learn more?

5. Can you change your learning style to accommodate varied methods of instruction?

References

Briggs, Katharine C. and Isabel Briggs Myers. *Myers-Briggs Type Indicator*. Palo Alto, Calif.: Consulting Psychologists Press, 1943.

Herrmann, Ned. Certification Workshop, Lake Lure, North Carolina, 1985. (Referenced materials are adaptations of workshop handouts.)

Jung, C. G. *Psychological Types*. New York: Harcourt Brace, 1923.

Kiersey, David and Marilyn Bates. *Please Understand Me*. Del Mar, Calif.: Prometheus Nemesis Books, 1978.

Restak, Richard M. *The Brain: The Last Frontier*. New York: Warner Books, 1979.

For Further Reading

Bigge, Morris L. *Learning Theories for Teachers*. New York: Harper & Row, 1976.

Buzan, Tony. *Use Both Sides of Your Brain*. New York: Dutton, 1974.

Edwards, Betty. *Drawing on the Right Side of the Brain: A Course in Enhancing Creativity and Artistic Confidence*. Los Angeles: J. P. Tarcher, 1979.

Hill, Winifred. *Principles of Learning: A Handbook of Applications*. Palo Alto, Calif.: Mayfield, 1982.

Lawrence, Gordon. *People Types and Tiger Stripes*. Center for Applications of Psychological Type, Gainesville, Florida, 1982.

Levy, Jerre. "Research Synthesis on Right and Left Hemisphere: We Think with Both Sides of the Brain." *Educational Leadership* (January 1983):66–71.

Myers, Isabel Briggs. *Gifts Differing*. Palo Alto, Calif.: Consulting Psychologists Press, 1980.

Springer, Sally P. and G. Deutsch. *Left Brain, Right Brain*. San Francisco: W. H. Freeman, 1981.

RETENTION AS A KEY TO SUCCESS

• • • • •

T he aim of this chapter is to help you improve your ability to remember a greater portion of what you read, see or hear. The goals are:

1. To help you understand more about the phenomenon called forgetting
2. To help you understand that remembering or retention is related to the way you learn or study
3. To help you learn how to improve your memory

Retention is not a process that automatically follows reading or hearing information. Rather, it is a process that must be developed. Development includes reducing the amount of forgetting and at the same time using techniques that enhance memory. In general, the ability to remember is related to a number of factors, some of which are:

1. Motivation
2. Need
3. Mental attitude
4. Time and effort

Your *motivation* must be appropriate and strong enough to provide you with the adequate drive to succeed. You must see a *need* for learning the material you are trying to learn. You must have the appropriate *mental attitude* — that is, you must intend to learn the information. Finally, you must be willing to expend the *time* and *effort* to learn the material well enough to remember it. Now let's take a closer look at retention and the factors related to it.

THE BRAIN AND MEMORY

As you probably know, the function of the brain, in the process of remembering is that of processing and storing information. When you see, hear, smell, touch, or taste, messages are sent to the brain. Once the message has been processed, it is sent to cells for storage. Items or messages are retrieved when the appropriate stimulus is presented; that is, a stimulus activates the appropriate brain cells and brings information out of storage. The brain, however, apparently does not store all the messages it receives. Why? We may speculate on at least two possible reasons. One is that the strength of the signal or the impact of the message is not strong enough. The second is that we may program our brains to accept certain information and reject other information. Over a period of years a person develops likes, dislikes, attitudes, opinions, and values formed from contacts with family, friends, and others. It is possible that, over the years, a person might be able to program the brain to accept and reject information, on the basis of likes and dislikes.

Now, how might this ability affect your success in college? You are wondering why you need to take a course in English literature or philosophy. After all, you are an engineering major — why do you need that stuff to be an engineer? Your negative attitude toward, or dislike of, literature or philosophy may make it very difficult for you to learn the material. The same might be true for the sociology major who questions a math course requirement. It is certainly true that we all prefer some subjects over others, but *there is a difference between preferring one area of study and programming ourselves to reject everything else.*

Let's assume for the moment that the brain does store the information you want to remember, but you still forget some of it. As stated earlier, stored information is recalled by an appropriate stimulus — that is, something that relates functionally to that stored information. It is possible that the information is not recalled because the appropriate stimulus is not present or the stimulus for recall is not strong enough. Another possibility for the failure to recall is the difference in situations at the time of storage and the time of recall. We usually learn in a *stimulus-related field,* which includes the specific stimulus and the context or situation in which the stimulus appears. For example, have you ever tried to remember the name of a childhood friend you haven't seen in years? The face may be vivid, but the name eludes you until you begin to visualize the friend's parents, brothers, sisters, and the house where he or she lived. If you then think of the name, you have used the context or the stimulus-related field to aid your memory.

The ability to recall learned material may function in much the same way. Learning does not occur in a vacuum. There is an association, a context, or a stimulus-related field. You may feel that you know material well, but the stimulus needed for a test may differ from the stimulus you used for storage, causing you some difficulty in answering the question. Perhaps you learned a principle of biology in a laboratory experiment, but when asked questions about the principle on a written test you are not able to respond because the context is so different. These are problems that may occur when you fail to associate and make use of the context or stimulus-related field, and they will be addressed in detail later in this chapter.

FORGETTING

Forgetting is a normal and natural event, though often bothersome to us. It is important and sometimes necessary that we forget or at least diminish the ease of recalling certain information. It is not important, for example, to remember the address and phone number of a friend who has moved. And even though you will never forget the death of a relative or friend, you will eventually be spared the pain of frequently recalling that event. Thus, forgetting has its negative and positive sides.

One of the first things to ask yourself when you have failed to remember material is if you ever really learned it in the first place. Simply reading or hearing something does not mean you learned it. How do you know when you have learned something? Have you learned something when you can recall it one week later, one month later, or one year later? Have you learned something when you can apply it in some way? What level of learning do you or your instructor desire? It is one thing to know information at a factual level and quite another to know how those facts relate or fit together (see Chapter 6 for information on levels of knowing). The level of knowing you reach and are satisfied with may not be the level expected by the instructor. You may not be able to display your knowledge to the instructor because it is at a different level. In the instructor's eyes, therefore, you may not have learned, and you may receive a low grade. You must define learning, at least while you are in college, in terms of the instructor's expectations.

In the late nineteenth century a German psychologist, Hermann Ebbinghaus, conducted research on memory and forgetting (1964). Many of his experiments involved the memorization of nonsense syllables (GIH, WUK, NAF, and so on) so that memory would not be influenced by previous learning. Ebbinghaus found that most forgetting occurs immediately after learning; after that, the forgetting process seems to slow down and we retain part of the material for a longer period of time. The process of forgetting *meaningful* material is not quite as rapid, but we probably forget 50 percent of meaningful material in about one week. The meaningfulness of the material is the important key. Even when the information is important, if it is not meaningful to you it is more difficult to remember. Can all subject areas or topics in subject areas be meaningful to you? Very unlikely, but before you make a snap decision, try to find ways to make the content of your courses meaningful. "How," you say, "can I make something meaningful that I don't like or worse, don't understand?" That is a fair and a tough question. The answer probably begins with your motivation in going to college. If that motivation is shaky—for example, there was nothing else to do—much of the content you are exposed to will not be meaningful. On the other hand, if your motivation is appropriate and the goal of getting a degree is strong, you will be able to generate some interest in those subjects that are not meaningful to you. Think about your long-range goal and keep it in mind when you find generating interest in a subject or a class heavy going.

CAUSES OF FORGETTING

A number of factors probably contribute to the process of forgetting. Perhaps the most common is some type of *stimulus interference,* which simply means that one bit of information interferes with another bit of information. Two stimuli are similar or two responses are similar and confusion comes about. To take a simple example, suppose you took Latin in high school and learned that the word *bellum* meant "war." Later, in college, you took Italian, saw the word *bella* and thought, "Hey, I know that." You soon learned, however, that *bella* in Italian means "beautiful." This type of interference can occur in almost any subject area—with dates and events in history, with properties of chemical elements, with economic principles, and so on.

Retroactive Inhibition

One type of stimulus interference that causes forgetting is known as *retroactive inhibition,* which simply means that recent learning interferes with recall of earlier learning. Suppose, for example, you learned in a military history course about a battle strategy used in the Civil War. Later you learned that a similar battle strategy was used in World War I. On an exam you are asked to describe how that strategy was used generally in wartime and you are able to describe the strategy in relation to World War I but forget about the Civil War. The later learning has interfered with the earlier learning. One possible way of overcoming the problem of retroactive inhibition is to connect the information. As you read your notes, make side notes to tie the two pieces of similar information together. In the memory example a simple note—"also used in the Civil War"—beside the notes about World War I would tie it together for you. Often the professor will mention, during a lecture, the relationship of similar material. When this happens, make a note of it.

Proactive Inhibition

Proactive inhibition is the situation in which earlier learning interferes with later learning. In our example, information about the Civil War might interfere with the information about World War I. The stimulus interference problem here is the opposite of retroactive inhibition. Correcting this type of interference, however, requires the same strategy, namely, to *connect* the material—note and learn the similarities and differences between the two events, facts, or situations.

Other Causes of Forgetting

Forgetting may simply be a function of failing to concentrate on the information when you hear or read it. How many times have you been introduced to someone and 30 seconds later cannot remember the person's name? This often happens to people who are more visual than auditory and is caused by the failure to concentrate on the name at the time it is heard. So it is with information you read or hear in college classes: It is possible to read words in a book or take notes in lecture mechanically, without concentrating on the meaning of the information. Everything goes in one ear (or eye) and out the other. Obviously it is difficult to take the time to concentrate or think about what is said in lecture. Remember, however, that you don't have to note down everything the instructor says. Once you develop the technique of *selective* notetaking, you will have time to think about information as it is presented. The same goes for reading: After reading a paragraph or two or a section, stop to think about what you read and the importance of the material.

Forgetting may also relate to how you feel about the material you are reading or hearing. If you do not like a subject area or some topic within a subject area, you will obviously find it more difficult to remember facts or principles in that area. Examine your reasons for not liking that subject. Is it because you don't do well in it? Do you have trouble thinking in the manner required to understand the content? Does the subject require more work than you are willing to give? Part of becoming a mature learner lies in accepting such situations as obstacles to overcome, problems to be solved. Learning to rise to a challenge can mean much more to you than success in college — it can mean success in life as well.

A final cause of forgetting is known as *information overload.* Absorbing or trying to absorb too much information in a short period of time can cause much confusion, frustration, stimulus interference, and forgetting. Information overload is a common problem for many people in business, particularly those in management positions. In college it can be a problem if:

1. You take too many classes or too many classes on the same day.
2. You also work and must deal with information on the job.
3. You try to study too much right before midterms or finals.

Information overload can also occur if you have a short attention span. Elementary teachers recognize that children have short attention spans and teach accordingly. Some people, however, seem to assume that adults do not have attention span problems, and unfortunately some of these people are university professors. In fact, *attention span,* or the ability to focus for extended periods of time, may be a problem at one time or another for all of us.

How is attention span related to information overload? Actually, it may not be functionally related; if you have a short attention span, however, almost any information coming at you will certainly seem like an overload! What is the nature of your attention span? Is it different in areas that you don't like, feel neutral about, or strongly like? Your answer to that question is (*probably*) yes. Can you control how much time you are able to sustain your *full* attention during a lecture? Probably not. Some professors do not recognize the attention span problem and do nothing to help, even though it is a relatively easy matter to break up an hour or hour-and-a-half lecture by asking students questions, using a bit of comic relief, using visuals, or a number of other ways. If, however, your professor does not use these techniques, you must provide for your attention span problem, if you have one, yourself. Some suggestions:

1. Work on becoming completely absorbed in the content of the course.

2. Try to take nonpreferred or difficult classes at a time of day when you are at your best. Some people are most alert during the morning hours, others at later times of the day. If multiple sections of a class are offered, take advantage of your peak times to choose the best hour for your concentration.

3. Try to take classes with professors who use teaching strategies such as discussions, questions, small groups, and the like that tend to improve the student's ability to pay attention.

4. Read the assignments before you attend lectures. Simply knowing something about the content of the lecture should improve your ability to listen closely.

5. If you become bored or feel your attention span fading, do something immediately. Stop for 10 seconds, close your eyes, and concentrate on getting back in the groove. Above all, don't let your mind wander to topics outside the classroom. Don't become involved in thoughts about a party, a date, a rock concert, a sporting event, or some other activity that may consume the remainder of the class period.

IMPROVING YOUR MEMORY

There is no sure way to improve memory that works for everyone. A technique's effectiveness may depend on whether you are a visual or an auditory learner. Visual learners tend to prefer pictures or images, whereas auditory learners prefer outlining, memorization, and logic. The following are general and specific suggestions for improving your ability to retain information. These ideas are starting points but may stimulate you to read further in some of the books listed at the end of the chapter.

1. Use spaced rather than massed learning.

One of the commonest practices among college students is that of studying for an exam the night before. These famous cram sessions may have one advantage; at least the information is fresh and students may absorb enough to get through the exam. But cram sessions lengthen for midterms and finals simply because there is more information to be learned. You will retain more from a number of shorter, evenly spaced study sessions than from one or two lengthy cram sessions. The cram session puts you in a position of having to absorb too much in a short period of time; you must be able to concentrate for long periods of time and thus handle the information overload problem. Can you do that?

To retain the largest percentage of information, you should review your lecture notes and textbooks frequently. Review your notes the day you make them, while the lecture is still fresh in your memory. You can also complete your notes during this review (see Chapter 5). If you have taken notes on the text or have hi-lited important information, try to review that material at least by the next day.

Following the initial review, try to review class notes and hi-lited text material two times each week. In these reviews include *self-recitation* — that is, read, recall, and ask yourself questions. Look at the questions at the end of the chapter. Can you answer them? Look at the syllabus for the course. Do you know the information the instructor expects you to know?

2. Transfer learning from short-term to long-term memory.

Short-term memory can range in time from a few minutes to a few days, but a few hours is probably the right length of time for most people. Short-term memory seems to have two useful purposes: (1) It is useful for remembering material to be used a few hours after it is learned. For example, if you review material just before an exam, you may remember some of it long enough to help you on the exam. (2) Short-term memory retains information long enough to transfer it into long-term memory. Unless you transfer information from short-term to long-term memory, it will not be of much value to you on exams. How is this transfer accomplished? Three activities will help you with this transfer.

    a. *Recite.* Probably the best technique for transferring information from short- to long-term memory is recitation. Some of the following may help you:

- Read a paragraph or two or a subsection in a chapter. Stop. Try to recall what you read. Recite the major points a few times.
- Ask yourself questions about the material.
- Relate the material to previously read material and your existing knowledge.
- Make a few flashcards related to major points and use these for study and recitation.
- Memorize a limited number of important facts and principles.
- Use the mnemonic or memory devices covered later in this chapter.

    b. Review frequently. As indicated earlier, frequent reviewing makes it possible for you to avoid massed study. One problem in massed study is that you don't allow yourself time to commit the material to long-term memory. Frequent review helps you remember material over a longer period of time.

3. Review before sleeping.

Some experts believe that you remember material better if you review it just before falling asleep. The reason you may remember better at this time is that less stimulus interference occurs while you are sleeping than when you are awake. This technique probably won't be helpful if that review is a cram session that tries to pack in too much material in too short a time. It is also likely that review before sleeping would be most useful for an early morning exam.

4. Intend to learn.

The mental attitude you have while studying is related to how well you remember. If you approach a study session with the attitude that you would rather be doing something else, your retention will be adversely affected. Mentally deciding that you *want* to learn — that you *intend* to learn the material will probably have a positive impact. Take a few minutes to relax and reflect on the importance of learning the material before you begin studying.

5. Develop specific objectives.

Another way to improve memory is to be clear about what you want or need to learn before you begin to read, listen, or review. The syllabus should be helpful in identifying what you should learn. Again, you can look at the questions at the end of the chapter to help identify the important material. Then write some objectives to guide your study. With your specific objectives in mind, you will absorb and store information related to those objectives more readily.

6. Develop diagrams or webs.

You probably remember diagramming sentences in high school. The purpose of diagramming sentences is to visualize the relationships among various parts of the sentence. You can develop *diagrams* or *webs* to help you remember various facts about a concept, idea, or piece of information. The two examples here show you how diagrams can be made. The first, which shows four characteristics of vitamin C, is less complex than the second on clouds. Diagrams of this nature can be as simple or as complex as you wish. In the cloud diagram, for example, you can list the three factors used here — altitude, composition, and form — and then list three or four additional points under each factor. Later you can add to the diagram if you need more detailed information.

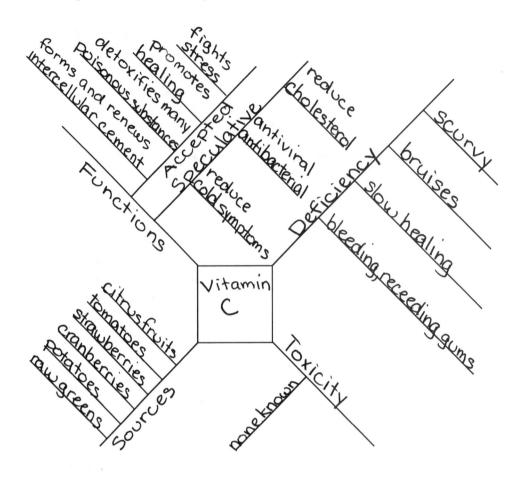

The vitamin C example simply shows four characteristics — functions, sources, toxicity, and deficiency — of vitamin C. Note that there is still controversy about all the functions of vitamin C, so they are divided into "accepted" and "speculative." Now try to web or diagram some information you need to remember.

7. Use mnemonic devices.

The previous techniques are primarily intended to help you improve retention as you read, listen, and study. The following techniques are to help you remember material you have studied. Remembering is not a passive act — it requires work, effort, and active participation with the information you want to remember, as you will see in some of the techniques presented here.

A *mnemonic device* is any technique that helps you to remember information. Some kinds of mnemonics seem artificial, others quite natural. For certain

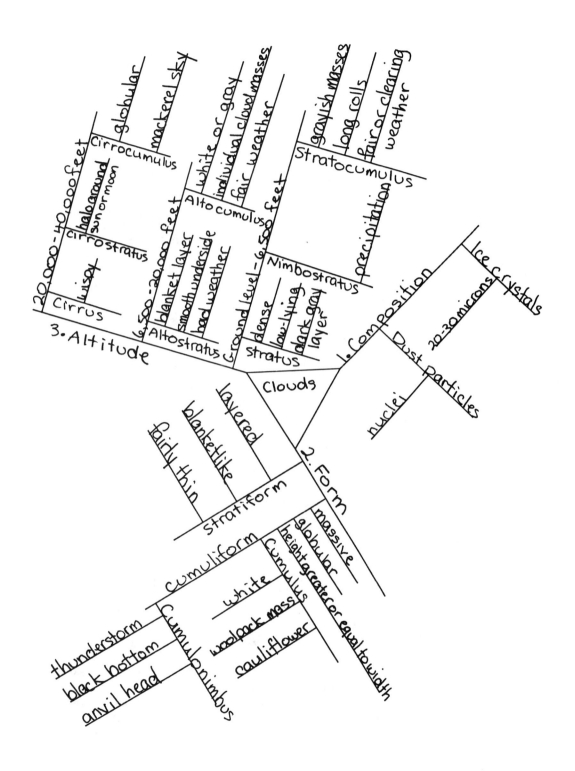

Clouds

3. Altitude

Cirrus — 20,000-40,000 feet — wispy

Cirrocumulus — globular — mackerel sky

Cirrostratus — halo around sun or moon

Altocumulus — 6,500-20,000 feet — white or gray — individual cloud masses — fair weather

Altostratus — blanket layer — smooth underside — bad weather

Nimbostratus — precipitation

Stratocumulus — grayish masses — long rolls — fair or clearing weather

Stratus — Ground level-6,500 feet — dense — low-lying — dark gray — layer

1. Composition

Ice Crystals

Dust Particles — 20-30 microns

nuclei

2. Form

Stratiform — layered — blanket like — fairly thin

Cumuliform — massive — globular — height greater or equal to width

Cumulus — white — woolpack mass — cauliflower

Cumulonimbus — thunderstorm — black bottom — anvil head

people, mnemonics take more time than they are worth; others learn effectively with these techniques. Mnemonics can range in difficulty from the
simple phrase, "In 1492 Columbus sailed the ocean blue," to very complicated schemes. Mnemonics here covers a broad range of memory techniques,
including visualization, memory pegs, picture-object association, and simple
mnemonics.

Visualization

Individuals vary in their ability to visualize. Such a variation might be attribut-
able to brain hemisphericity preference; right-preference persons tend to use
visualization techniques more than left-preference persons. (A recent conversation with a math major revealed that she did not use visualization and did not
seem to know how it might work.) Some people are able to use a visualization
process effectively; for others, though it is not natural, it can certainly be
learned. Try looking at pictures, scenery, objects. Then close your eyes and
recreate in your mind what you saw. Practice this type of activity frequently
and you can develop improved recall through visualization.

Effective visualization is not an automatic process. You must do more than
visualize — you must associate the items in the mental picture with each other
and with information you already know. For example, if you look at an un-
signed painting by Rembrandt but are able to identify the painter, you have
associated something in the painting with something you already knew. Such
associations can be very logical, normal, and natural or they can be illogical,
bizarre, and perhaps abnormal. Because we all have tremendous amounts of
information stored in our brain, associative prediction is very difficult. Ink blot
tests are a good illustration of that phenomenon: Some people see very realistic
designs to which they attach labels such as butterfly or two bears standing on
their back legs; others see bizarre patterns. So it is not possible for us to suggest
the type of associations you might or should develop between the information
you want to learn and your own experience. Try some *free associating* — that
is, consider whatever pops into your brain as you think about the information
to be remembered. Then determine if any kind of relationship exists between
the free-associated thought and the information and use this relationship as a
memory aid. Relaxing and removing extraneous thoughts from your brain will
usually help. Finally, after you have relaxed, associated, and allowed the
association to function, you must recite or think through the association
several times to imprint it thoroughly.

Some basketball players mentally rehearse every movement involved in a
shot. They visualize their jump, releasing the ball, the path of the ball toward
the hoop, and the ball going through the hoop. Keeping that mental picture
intact provides a type of automatic feedback that helps provide continued
success. The Olympic champion diver Greg Louganis visualizes his entire dive
before he dives. This visual imprint takes over and controls the body to bring
about the visualized dive.

The same process can help you learn and retain the material you have learned. For example, suppose you needed to memorize Robert Frost's poem "Birches." You could easily picture the descriptions in the poem. Picture white birch trees bending from left to right, a boy swinging on birch trees, ice covered limbs, the sun reflecting off the ice. These items are fairly easy to visualize because the poet has provided visual descriptions of them. Other information may not be as easy to visualize because the language involved may not be vivid or the information may be abstract. The trick is to attach descriptive language or to relate the abstraction to concrete objects. The following are examples of mental pictures that may help you remember less descriptive material.

1. To remember the difference between a bull and a bear stock market, first visualize a Dow-Jones indicator similar to a large thermometer. Further picture a seat at the bottom of the indicator and a seat at the top of the indicator. For a rising market, picture the bull sitting on the seat at the bottom pushing the indicator up. For a declining market, picture a bear sitting in the top seat holding the indicator down.

2. During periods of inflation, persons on fixed incomes suffer more than those whose salaries can be increased to allow for inflation. Picture an elderly couple on a fixed income looking at an inflation index of ten percent and an empty cupboard.

3. During periods of inflation, people tend to purchase items they don't yet need in order to avoid paying a higher price for them later. Can you think of a mental picture to fit this situation?

4. To remember the relationship of volume, pressure, and temperature, think of an inflated balloon on a radiator and the same balloon in the refrigerator. Visualize the balloon expanding on the radiator and shrinking in the refrigerator.

Picture-Object Association.   One of the earliest visualization techniques is called the *method of loci,* attributed to an ancient Greek named Simonides. While attending a gathering of many people, Simonides was called outside and while he was outside the building collapsed killing everyone inside. The bodies could not be identified because they were badly crushed. However, Simonides using his visual memory was able to identify the dead by where they were sitting and their relationship to others, the room, etc. This method involves associating items, objects, events, etc. with the surrounding environment and with each other.

You can create a picture by associating items or facts you want to remember with concrete objects or even with abstractions. Let's suppose you need to remember the names, in order of descending size, of the ten largest (in square miles) states in the United States. Try something like this.

Picture a plate of baked Alaska setting on a table. Sticking in the baked Alaska is one point of a large red star, the symbol of Texaco. Hanging on another point of the star is a sign that has the word "calories" written on it. A Monty Python character is swinging from another point on the star. Hanging on another point is a large hat—a sombrero with the words "new not old" printed on it. On top of the sombrero is a gila monster holding a deck of cards and a stack of poker chips.

Now, what are the first seven states? What are the key words which can be used to identify the first seven states. The baked Alaska is obviously Alaska, our starting point. The Texaco star represents Texas and the calories stand for California. Monty Python should remind you of Montana. The sombrero is a symbol of Mexico—but the "New" Mexico, not the old one. The gila monster is a symbol of Arizona; the cards and chips suggest Nevada. Can you add the next three largest states—Colorado, Wyoming, and Oregon—to the picture? You can create this type of story with many sets of facts you want to remember.

Memory Pegs.   Some memory experts advocate using the same set of *memory pegs* for anything you want to remember. This method involves learning ten words in association with the numbers 1 through 10. This association is suggested because you will never forget those numbers. The words associated with the numbers usually rhyme with the numbers because rhyming words are easy to remember. They are typically nouns; some experts, however, use one or two verbs. Perhaps the real trick is to select words that can be used as both nouns or verbs, such as *score* and *fix*. Using this system, you can remember lists, sets of facts, numbers, and other types of information over and over again. The associations may seem outlandish or bizarre, but they work for some people. Let's try the method using the following pegs:

One	is	Bun
Two	is	Crew
Three	is	Tree
Four	is	Score
Five	is	Chive
Six	is	Fix
Seven	is	Heaven
Eight	is	Date
Nine	is	Shrine
Ten	is	Den

Now, how does it work? Suppose you need to remember the number 92748. First, what are the words pegged to these digits? They are *shrine, crew, heaven, score,* and *date.* Now make up a sentence using these words. For example:

The *shrine* for the *crew* of the Enterprise, who are in *heaven,* will *score* well with the public when the committee sets a *date* to begin construction.

Although some people find it easier to memorize the number than to create a sentence and remember the sentence, the key here is to make associations with items that you know well or that are vivid in your memory. Now you try one. How about pi, 3.1415826 . . . ? See if you can make up a sentence to remember pi to four places.

This system is probably useful for remembering long lists of facts if the story or sentence is something you can relate to easily, that is, something familiar to you. Now try making your own set of memory pegs. Then memorize them and apply the system to a set of facts you need to remember.

Simple Mnemonics

You have probably used *simple mnemonics* many times. The most common way is either to reduce the amount of content you have to remember to something very short and memorize that or to expand the information into a story, as indicated earlier. Some examples are:

Men Very Early Make Jugs Serve Useful and Numerous Purposes.

Richard of York Gains Battles in Vain.

The first jingle is a way to remember the names of the planets and the second our friends in physics suggest is a way to remember the order of colors in the spectrum—red, orange, yellow, green, blue, indigo, and violet.

To remember people's names, try to associate the features of a person with something that will help you recall the name. For example, let's suppose you meet a man named Hackett and it is important that you remember his name. Suppose Mr. Hackett is a large burly man who looks like he could *hack* his way through a thick*et.* So now you have his name.

There is little point in providing you with more readymade examples because they won't fit your needs. If you want to use this type of memory device, let your imagination and creativity take over. Think up realistic or bizarre or absurd relationships—whatever you feel is most useful to you. Try some of these methods and evaluate their usefulness to you.

Review

Effective retention of information is not an automatic process—it requires hard work on your part. Retention can, however, be enhanced in a number of ways. Even though forgetting is a normal and natural process, you can reduce the amount you forget and thus improve the amount you remember. Cutting down the stimulus interference that increases forgetting can, at the same time, increase your retention. Try to avoid unwittingly programming yourself to forget by developing negative attitudes toward certain types of content or information.

Some specific tips for increasing the amount of information you retain — that is, for improving your memory — are:

1. Use spaced rather than massed study.

2. Use processes to help you transfer information from short-term to long-term memory.

3. Review before sleeping.

4. Make a conscious decision to learn the material rather than just studying mechanically.

5. Develop objectives to guide your study.

6. Use mnemonic devices such as visualization, association, and memory pegs to enhance your memory.

Review Questions

1. How can you program your brain to store information?

2. How do you know when you have learned?

3. What is retroactive inhibition? Proactive inhibition?

4. What are two other causes of forgetting?

5. What is a mnemonic device?

6. What are two ways you can improve your memory using visualization?

7. How can you use picture-object association?

8. Memory pegs would be most useful for remembering what kinds of information?

References

Ebbinghaus, Hermann. *Memory: A Contribution to Experimental Psychology.* Mineola, N.Y.: Dover, 1964.

For Further Reading

Gallant, Roy A. *Memory: How It Works and How to Improve It*. New York: Four Winds Press, 1980.

Grunebery, M. M. and P. E. Morris. *Applied Problems in Memory*. London: Academic Press, 1979.

Klatzky, Roberta. *Human Memory: Structures and Processes*. San Francisco: W. H. Freeman, 1975.

McGaugh, James L. *Learning and Memory: An Introduction*. San Francisco: Albion, 1973.

Montgomery, Robert Lee. *Memory Made Easy*. New York: AMACOM, 1979.

Underwood, Geoffrey. *Attention and Memory*. Oxford: Pergamon Press, 1976.

ACTIVE
LISTENING AS A
KEY TO SUCCESS

I f you think about what you do most of the time you're in a classroom, you may think you don't do much. After all, in many college classes you'll take, the professor lectures and you sit quietly taking notes. But, in fact, you are doing a great deal of work—or least you should be, because you're engaged in the extremely important task of *listening*. The goals of this chapter are:

1. To understand the importance of effective listening to the classroom communication process
2. To understand the importance of effective listening to your academic success
3. To recognize the problems and distractions that often cause you to be an ineffective listener
4. To develop techniques and strategies to enhance your listening skills

The importance of listening to your educational success can be illustrated by looking at a simplified model of the human communication process (Berlo, 1960):

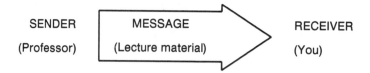

Many people think that "communication" only takes place when somebody says something, when your professor begins to present the lecture materials aloud. But that only tells part of the story. For communication actually to take place, there has to be a recipient of the speaker's message; in this case, you, as student, serve to receive the lecture materials presented by your professor. Since it is not possible to teach in and to an empty classroom, *you are a critical part of the classroom communication process, and the effectiveness of classroom communication will depend largely upon how effectively you listen.*

COMMUNICATION NEEDS YOU!

In fact, the best lecture or class discussion has no value if people do not listen. The best teacher you will ever meet has his or her classroom achievement determined largely by how effectively the students listen to that teacher.

The communication process does not take place without a receiver of information; classroom communication is incomplete (and totally ineffective) without you as a listener.

· · · · · · · · · ·

HOW CAN I TEACH IF THEY DON'T LISTEN?
HOW CAN THEY LEARN IF THEY DON'T LISTEN?

· · · · · · · · · ·

We tend not to think a great deal about listening because we do so much of it. Studies conducted from the 1920s to the present have attempted to determine how much of our daily activities are spent listening to someone else (Weaver, 1972). Though the percentages vary a bit from one study to another, in general here is how *you* spend your day involved in communication:

Writing = 10%

Reading = 15%

Talking/Speaking = 30%

LISTENING = 45%

Nearly one-half of your daily communication activities consists of listening, more than reading and writing combined, a fact that is especially compelling when you visualize these differences in a simple pie chart:

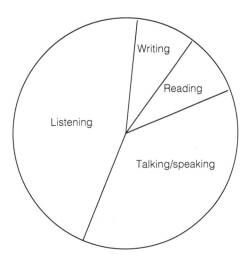

Now you can easily see how important listening is as a part of your overall communication behavior and why you need to be concerned about developing your skills as an effective listener.

Unfortunately, most of us are not effective listeners most of the time, regardless of situation. In fact—and here's the scary part—the average person only listens with 25 percent efficiency, meaning that we remember and retain less information than the small percentage we are able to take in initially! Apply that percentage to your performance in the classroom. If you listen at only 25 percent efficiency, do you understand why there are some classroom materials you somehow did not recall?

• • • • • • • • • •

IS ANYONE OUT THERE LISTENING?

• • • • • • • • • •

Every teacher in the world has had this conversation with an irate student after returning an important exam:

STUDENT: I can't believe it! I got a C on this test and I studied my tail off!

TEACHER: Maybe you studied the wrong material. Or maybe you didn't read all the questions quite carefully enough.

STUDENT: No. The problem is that you asked stuff that's not in the book. You didn't talk about it in class, either. That's not fair!

TEACHER: Show me the questions on the exam you think aren't fair.

STUDENT: Here, take a look at the questions I've circled. That stuff isn't in the book and you didn't discuss them, either.

TEACHER: I'm sorry, but the information for those test questions was given during my lectures.

STUDENT: There's no way! I've been here every time. I've never missed a class!

Was the student lying? Did he or she miss some classes where those test materials were explained? Maybe not, for it is very possible that that student was in class but did not effectively listen, thereby missing the information needed to do well on the exam. Just being physically present does not guarantee that you'll hear everything you ought to.

• • • • • • • • • •

IF I DIDN'T HEAR IT, AM I HELD RESPONSIBLE FOR IT?

• • • • • • • • • •

If your listening habits could be charted like an EKG, your listening chart probably would look like this:

Your listening/non-listening behavior

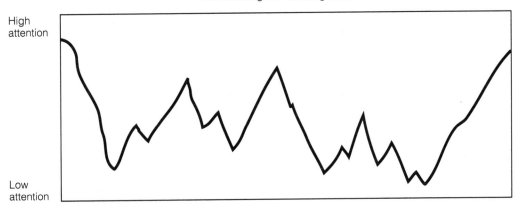

High
attention

Low
attention

We do not listen in a consistent pattern; also, unfortunately, we do not pay attention at the same or consistent level all the way through the message. Instead, our listening behavior is characterized by a series of *peaks* and *valleys,* times when we're listening rather carefully (peaks) and times when we're really not listening at all (valleys).

In the classroom, you tend to listen most carefully at the beginning of lectures to (1) see what today's information is going to be about, and (2) determine if the material is going to be interesting or boring. Once you've made those determinations, you'll tend (unless you consciously and overtly fight this tendency) to let your mind wander to other matters: that nice-looking guy or girl sitting next to you, what you plan to do for lunch or dinner, hassles you're having at home or work, and the like. You are there in the classroom and you are semiconscious of what's going on around you, but your mind and your thoughts are not on the information being presented by your teacher.

This phenomenon is known as *out-listening,* meaning that you really are not listening to the lecture at all. Throughout the class session, you tune the lecture in and out, occasionally listening to what is being said, at other times drifting a million miles away in your thoughts. This up-and-down pattern explains why students miss important information presented by the teacher — even when the teacher is doing the best possible job in presenting lecture materials. We allow ourselves to be distracted away from the lecture information, and that is why we have such an overall poor listening efficiency.

• • • • • • • • • •

I WISH I COULD CHOOSE WHAT TO FORGET!

• • • • • • • • • •

Our poor listening habits also take place in other types of classroom situations, including class discussions and individual presentations. Because it is so easy *not* to listen, we often do just that, missing information presented by our fellow students as well as by our teachers. You might have experienced this phenomenon yourself:

YOU: That concludes my presentation. Are there any questions about my report?

OTHER STUDENT: Yes, what do you think will be the long-term effects of the growing budget deficits of the United States?

YOU: Well, uh, I covered that in the first part. Do you want me to repeat what I've already said?

OTHER STUDENT: What did you say?

You might have made your analysis and information extremely clear, but that student was out-listening at the time and he/she missed the point altogether. Thus, poor listening doesn't occur only during classroom lectures; poor listening occurs in every type of classroom setting.

• • •
> **SELF-DIAGNOSTIC**
>
> Recall a conversation you had with a friend today. How much of that conversation can you recall? Can you remember even half of it? If you honestly assess your own listening habits and skills, you'll find there's plenty of room for improvement.

FACTORS CONTRIBUTING TO POOR LISTENING

A number of factors can cause us not to listen effectively, many of which we can overcome if we make the effort to deal with them. Let's look at several of these.

Physical Conditions

Sometimes you'll find yourself in a classroom that makes listening difficult. If the room is too hot or too cold, you'll be more concerned with your physical comfort than with listening to what's going on.

• • • • • • • • • •

HOW CAN I LISTEN WHEN MY FEET ARE NUMB?

• • • • • • • • • •

Or you'll be so far away from the teacher (large mass lecture halls often seat several hundred students in the same class) that it's easy *not* to pay attention to the lecture.

• • • • • • • • • •

CAN ANYONE HERE EVEN SEE THE TEACHER?

• • • • • • • • • •

You also will be affected by distracting noise both inside and outside the classroom, such as other students talking, people walking past the classroom door, airplanes flying overhead, someone cutting grass just outside the window, and so on.

In such circumstances, you must make a *conscious* effort not to allow yourself to be distracted away from the classroom activity. Even though it is very easy *not* to pay attention, if you want to be as successful a student as possible, it is crucial you make every effort to tune out distracting physical problems. Making that effort will allow you to succeed.

To help you overcome such physical distractions in class, constantly think about what has just been said. How does that information relate to what was said earlier? How does that information relate to information in the textbook and in other sources? By reviewing and analyzing classroom information throughout the class period, you'll find it easier not to be distracted because your concentration is focused on the task at hand.

Preconceived Attitudes

Every college student has to take a number of classes that he or she doesn't want to. If you're a chemistry major, you may not want to take a course in English composition. A journalism major may grumble about having to take a math class. A business major may object to having to enroll in an art history class. And on and on. Every student, including you, will be unhappy about having to take some class or another, and your negative attitude can affect how effectively or ineffectively you will listen in the classroom.

Consider this example:

STUDENT   (*thinking silently*): I can't believe I have to take this stupid class! This has nothing to do with my major. What a waste of time and my hard-earned money!

TEACHER: Today we're going to examine the philosophical foundations of democratic government.

STUDENT   (*still thinking silently*): Who cares? This is going to be as exciting as watching a bridge rust. Why do I have to be here?

How effectively do you think that student is going to listen? Probably not very effectively at all, and this will create a vicious circle: Because of poor listening caused by the student's reluctance to be in that class, he or she will not do well on the first exam. The bad grade in turn will make the student even more resistant, causing the listening level to drop farther, resulting in even poorer grades on the following exams. The situation goes from bad to worse very quickly.

POOR LISTENING⟶ POOR GRADES⟶ POORER LISTENING⟶ POORER GRADES

Granted, you, like every student, will be required to take classes you aren't excited about (you may be enrolled in one of them right now!), and you'll grumble about not having any choice in the matter. Instead of carrying on and bemoaning your fate, however, why not make the best of it? As long as you have to take that class, why not learn as much as possible and get the best grade you can? Don't let the system turn you into an ineffective listener and a poor performer. Make the best effort you can, work at paying close attention in each class session, and you'll be rewarded with a higher grade than you thought possible. And we'll bet you'll enjoy and learn more from that class than you thought you would. Don't let a negative attitude prevent you from achieving academic success.

• • • • • • • • • •

WHO'S GOING TO WIN — YOU OR THE SYSTEM?

• • • • • • • • •

Communication Barriers

This area is fraught with possible problems. For one thing, you are able to think at a rate much faster than any person can talk. The average speaker has a delivery rate of around 200 words per minute, but you can think at four times that rate, almost 800 words per minute. That's why it's possible for you to "listen" to someone while thinking about some completely unrelated topic. Your mind processes information faster than people speak to you, providing a built-in distraction to effective listening. That's why it is so important for you to concentrate on a person's message, to listen carefully and critically, thereby reducing the amount of information lost because of the rate differences between speaking and thinking.

- - -

SELF-DIAGNOSTIC

Recall a recent conversation you had with someone — a friend, teacher, a parent. As you remember what you spoke about, try to recall the other thoughts that went through your mind during your conversation.

The next time you have a conversation or are in a classroom listening to a lecture, keep track of the times your mind wanders away from the topic. See the problem?

As in dealing with physical barriers to effective listening, you can help minimize the speaking-thinking rate difference by constantly reviewing and reflecting on what you've heard in the classroom. By comparing what you have just heard with information learned earlier (from the teacher, the textbook, or another source), you can gain a better understanding of that information as well as reducing the distractions inherent in the gap between speaking and thinking.

We also have difficulty listening to someone who either (1) presents material in an uninteresting manner or who (2) has an unpleasant speaking voice or distracting delivery mannerisms (Sayer and Rickert, 1985). If the teacher reads his or her lecture notes without looking up, talks to the chalkboard instead of the class, or obviously could care less about the information in the lecture, those are invitations *not* to listen. Sure, it would be great if every teacher lectured with enthusiasm, were a top-notch public speaker, and realized that other methods of teaching exist besides straight lecturing, but that is not the case. You must, however, resist the temptation to say to yourself, "It's not my fault this teacher's boring!" and take a mental nap. You still have the responsibility of listening — not an easy task, but one you must shoulder if you are to succeed in the classroom.

• • • • • • • • • •

WHY SHOULD I LISTEN WHEN MY TEACHER DOESN'T CARE ABOUT THIS CLASS? WHY SHOULD I LISTEN IF THE TEACHER DOESN'T CARE?

• • • • • • • • • •

In this kind of classroom situation, it becomes a matter of will on your part, a determination to gain something from even the most boring, poorly prepared speaker. Most of the time we tend to cop out, to not listen, but that doesn't absolve you of your responsibilities as a student, regardless of how rotten the lecturer might be.

Look at it this way. Most students will take the easy way out and blame the teacher for a boring class, saying things like, "Nobody could listen to a jerk like that!" But those same students still have to complete exams, turn in homework assignments, write papers, and so on, and then they'll blame the teacher for their poor grades. It's easy to blame the teacher, but you are the one getting the grade. Instead of reacting defensively to poor communication, be aggressive in a positive way. Decide to get something of value from even the most boring lecturer. Concentrate upon the teacher's message no matter how poorly it may be presented. Let others grumble and complain; you should try to profit actively from every class session. Again, it's a matter of will on your part.

Personal Emotional Factors

Did you ever have a "bad day"? Did you ever have a day when your stomach felt queasy, when you had a nasty argument with a friend, or when the whole world was against you? Sure you have, we all do, and those bad days can hamper our classroom listening habits.

If you've just had a knockdown-dragout fight with someone, you'll probably sit in class rehashing that argument over and over in your mind, and you won't pay attention to or listen to what's going on in the classroom. That is very human, but does rehashing the fight change anything? Will thinking about the hassles of your job eliminate those hassles? Of course not. But allowing your distress to get in the way of effective listening will create even greater problems for you in that class. You must make the effort, difficult as it is, to keep your out-of-class problems right there — out of the classroom.

Personal Physical Factors

Just like the emotional factors we looked at, your physical state will affect your overall listening behavior. If you are fatigued, you may find yourself nodding off during lectures, and it's very difficult to listen well while you're asleep! Or if you haven't eaten for several hours, you'll be more concerned with your growling stomach than with the information presented in class.

• • • • • • • • •

MY STOMACH RUMBLED SO BADLY I MISSED EVERY OTHER WORD!

• • • • • • • • •

Besides trying to control the obvious (get enough rest; eat balanced meals at appropriate times), you ought to consider physical factors when planning your class schedule. Although it may appear attractive to schedule five classes in a row to "get them out of the way" by early afternoon, think what that schedule will do to you physically. By the time the fifth class rolls around, you'll be punchy and in a zombie-like state, and your listening efficiency will be below measureable standards.

Just as an athlete learns that pacing is important, the same is true for the classroom student. Taking all your classes in one day is no great bargain if fatigue makes you an ineffective listener, and your grades very well may suffer from this self-induced physical strain.

IMPROVING LISTENING SKILLS

Now that we've considered five of the most common barriers to effective listening in the classroom, let's see what can be done to improve your listening habits. Overall, as we've stressed, a large part of the listening process depends upon your own willingness to be a better listener than you have been up to now. *You* must make the commitment to better listening.

• • • • • • • • •

LISTENING IS A PERSONAL MATTER: YOU MUST TAKE CHARGE

• • • • • • • • •

1. Be physically prepared.

The first skill to develop is your actual physical preparation for listening, your readiness to pay careful attention to the different classroom activities (lecture information, student reports, class discussion). The next time you go to class, look at the other students and you'll see something very much like this: When the teacher walks in, many students are busy talking with each other, too busy to even notice that the teacher has arrived. As the lecture begins, a few students continue chatting; others finally decide to get comfortable, removing coats, sliding back in their seats. A few minutes later, some students can be seen digging around for a pen and paper to take notes. A few students continue their own conversations.

Instead of being physically prepared to listen, many students get caught up with other matters and completely miss the first several minutes of the lecture.

Remember that irate student who was certain some test materials had not been presented in lecture? It's possible the student missed that information because he or she was not physically prepared to listen before the lecture began. By the time the student began to listen, that information had already been presented.

• • • • • • • • • •

IT'S HARD TO REMEMBER WHAT YOU DON'T HEAR.

• • • • • • • • • •

You don't want to make the same mistake. You want to be ready to listen *before* the teacher begins speaking. If you need to take off your coat or roll up your sleeves to get comfortable, do it before class begins. If you intend to take notes, have your pen or pencil and paper ready to go before the teacher starts giving out information. And, if you have a tendency to be easily distracted, sit up front to cut down on the distractions affecting you. In short, you should be ready to participate in class *before* the class begins.

Similarly, because effective listening must be a class-long activity, you do not want to stop listening before the instruction stops. But you've witnessed this scene before: With five minutes to go in class, students begin to get ready to leave. Notebooks are closed, pens are put away, jackets and shoes are put on. Then some of the students slide forward in their chairs, poised to bolt from the room the moment class is dismissed. When the teacher says, "That's it for today," they lurch from their chairs like racehorses lest they be the last to leave the room.

As with the earlier example, students who stop listening before the class ends may miss important information, homework responsibilities, and reading assignments. This type of behavior is also a surefire way to get on the bad side of the teacher. If your class is sixty minutes long, you should be prepared to listen for the full sixty minutes.

2. Scrutinize the information critically.

The more time you spend in a classroom, the more it seems you do nothing except take notes, writing down the important pieces of information your teacher hands down. But you must do more than that. Certainly, you need to take notes, for that information is generally designed to supplement material in the textbook and to give you a more complete understanding of the subject matter of the course. Taking notes, however, does not mean that you have to suspend all your thought processes and turn yourself into an automatic copy machine.

Listening is not a passive activity; listening should form a very active part of the communication process. As information is presented to you, *reflect* on what has been said — even as you're recording that information in your notes. Does that information make sense to you? Do you understand what has been said? Does that information agree with what the teacher has said before and/or what is written in your textbook? Or does that information contradict the new information?

MARK: Brenda, can I look at your Introduction to Philosophy notes? I'm studying for our exam, but my notes aren't helping me much.

BRENDA: What's the problem? Cut too many classes?

MARK: No, that's not it. Some of my notes don't make sense. I can't figure out what the prof said, and some of the stuff isn't the same as in the book. The numbers and other things are different. I don't know which stuff to study.

If Mark had listened critically in class instead of just writing down everything he heard, he wouldn't be in the predicament he's in now. If you listen critically and carefully to what is said, you can ask for clarification and explanation then, right during class. But Mark did not listen critically, and now he has no way of determining what his notes mean and what he should study. Critical listening can solve problems before they occur; critical listening makes you an active part of the communication process; *critical listening makes you a better student.*

3. Control your prejudices.

Probably one of the greatest hassles you have in college is being required to take a number of classes you really don't want to take. Or you'll wind up getting a class with an instructor you just know is going to be mean/horrible/rotten/intolerable. Under these circumstances it's natural to have a negative attitude about the class or instructor.

• • • • • • • • •

WHY DID I HAVE TO GET THAT JERK FOR AN INSTRUCTOR?

• • • • • • • • •

Instead of allowing this negative attitude to destroy your effective listening activity, control your prejudices and listen as carefully and critically as if this course were your very favorite. Although this will not solve all your problems (you still may dislike the class), at least you will not suffer academically. That class still has an impact on your overall education; it still counts on your grade point average. If you decide to tune out as a protest against having to take a class, only you will suffer in the end.

Control your prejudices so you can listen effectively in all classes, because final grades and grade point averages do not make distinctions between the classes you wanted to take and those you did not.

4. Listen appropriately for information.

The key to this listening skill is the idea of listening *appropriately.* Not all classes are the same, and so your listening habits cannot be the same, either. For example, an introductory class in American history will present a great deal of specific information such as dates, places, and names. In that class, therefore, you will want to concentrate upon listening for those pieces of important factual information. On an exam you will need to know when the Boston Tea Party took place—a very specific historical fact.

A course such as Theories of Mass Communication, however, will be more conceptually oriented than that history class. Facts per se will not be as important. Instead, a theoretically based class will emphasize broader concepts and philosophies, and you'll have to adjust your listening behavior accordingly. Just as a shirt will not fit all people, your listening behavior must be modified for each type of information you receive.

• • • • • • • • • •

LISTENING MUST BE RELATIVE AND CONTENT-SPECIFIC.

• • • • • • • • • •

5. Perceive relationships.

The final essential skill we will consider in developing your listening habits is identifying the relationships among the materials you study, a necessary skill if you are to gain the most you can from your studies. These content relationships exist both within each particular course *and* between different courses.

When you listen to classroom information, you want to review mentally what went before in relation to what you are hearing in the present. Hopefully, each lecture has been organized so that all parts of it hang together logically. Regardless, you need to think about the interconnections, and you have to listen actively and carefully to make that determination. Not only will you have a better understanding of the information by making logical connections between parts of the material, but you'll have a much better perspective on the overall content of the course. Instead of regarding information simply as floating bits of names, places, statistics, theories, and so on, developing content relationships through effective listening allows you to see the big picture. To paraphrase an old saying: Too many students don't see the forest because they're too concerned with looking at individual trees. You want to see both —the individual trees *and* the forest created by all the trees together. American history, for example, is not a jumble of discrete people or events; it is an interlocking relationship of people and events over time.

• • • • • • • • • •

ANYONE CAN SEE A BOOK, BUT LIFE IS REALLY A LIBRARY.

• • • • • • • • • •

Similarly, though you will take between forty and fifty courses throughout your college career, relationships exist between those courses, and you should perceive them. Not only will those cross-course relationships make you better able to understand information within each course, they will also allow you to have a better, more holistic view of the material you study in all your courses.

If you will make the effort, finally, to become an effective and efficient listener, you will receive a great payoff academically. You will get more from your classes than before by being better informed, better able to identify informational relationships, and better prepared to apply that information — both in the classroom and in your personal and professional life.

Review

Although listening is the commonest of daily communication activities, most people have very poor listening skills and generally have a listening recall efficiency of only 25 percent. Five factors often contribute to poor listening habits: (1) Physical conditions distract you, (2) preconceived negative attitudes cause you not to listen, (3) various communication barriers inhibit careful and thoughtful listening, both (4) personal emotional factors, and (5) personal physical factors can interfere with listening to the messages of others.

To improve your listening, you need to concentrate on the development and refinement of five skills: (1) Be prepared to listen before the message starts, (2) critically scrutinize information, (3) control your prejudices, (4) employ the appropriate manner of listening for each message; and (5) perceive the relationships among informational materials.

Review Questions

1. What percentage of your normal day do you spend engaged in listening to others? Keep a record for a few days to determine for yourself how important effective listening is to you.

2. Do you think you now listen effectively in the classroom? Have there been times when you've not done well on assignments or exams because you didn't listen effectively?

3. Do others in your classes listen at the same level of efficiency as you? After class one day, compare and contrast your notes with those of another student. Can you tell who did the better job of listening?

References

Berlo, David K. *The Process of Communication*. New York: Holt, Rinehart and Winston, 1960.

Sayer, James E. and William E. Rickert. *Functional Speech Communication: Theory and Practice in Oral Communication.* Dubuque, Iowa: Kendall/Hunt, 1985.

Weaver, Carl H. *Human Listening: Processes and Behavior.* New York: Bobbs-Merrill, 1972.

For Further Reading

Adler, Ronald B. and Neil Towne. *Looking Out/Looking In.* 5th ed. New York: Holt, Rinehart and Winston, 1987.

Barker, Larry L. *Listening Behavior.* Englewood Cliffs, N.J.: Prentice-Hall, 1971.

Brooks, William D. and Philip Emmert. *Interpersonal Communication.* Dubuque, Iowa: W. C. Brown and Company, 1980.

Steil, Lyman K., Barker, Larry L. and Kittie W. Watson. *Effective Listening.* Reading, Mass.: Addison-Wesley, 1983.

NOTETAKING AS A KEY TO SUCCESS

• • • • •

Effective notetaking is an absolutely essential skill for success in college. Very few of us have the ability to remember a significant amount of material we have heard. As stated previously, the average person remembers only about 50 percent of orally delivered material after one week. So unless you are one of the few with a superior memory, you must learn to be a good notetaker.

Notetaking, however, is not an isolated skill. It depends on yet another skill—listening. Effective listening may or may not make you a good notetaker, but poor listening will almost certainly prevent effective notetaking. Successful notetaking reflects your ability to distinguish between what is and what is not important (listening and analysis) as well as your skill in recording information that can be used later.

The goals of this chapter are:

1. To help you identify your skill as a notetaker
2. To help you improve your notetaking on lectures
3. To help you improve your notetaking on books
4. To help you improve your use of notes

This chapter will probably be most useful to you if you study it in conjunction with Chapters 4 and 6. Chapter 4 will help you to improve your listening skills and thus your notetaking. Chapter 6 will help you take notes from books because it contains suggestions for identifying important material.

MISCONCEPTIONS ABOUT NOTETAKING

As a way of introducing you to the topic, let's explore some common misconceptions about notetaking.

• • • • • • • • • •

MISCONCEPTION 1:

Write down everything the professor says.

• • • • • • • • • •

Everything the professor says is not of equal importance—there is always some chaff among the wheat, some noncritical material mixed in with the critical. Further, professors will not test you on everything covered in class. Even if you wanted or needed to make comprehensive notes, you simply could not write fast enough; try instead to select key and relevant material from the lecture. The hidden danger in trying to record everything is that you will focus only on writing instead of on the dual function of listening *and* taking notes.

Trying to catch everything causes you to listen for *words rather than meaning*. You are so busy writing words that their meaning may pass you by. You must learn to take in the critical content and meaning along with the words you write; otherwise, your notes may be useless. How can you learn to identify important material or what the instructor considers important material? Consider the following techniques.

1. Read the text material and any assigned supplementary material.

Many professors organize the text and outside readings to correspond with the lecture. Material that appears both places — in the text or outside readings and also in the lecture — is very likely to be significant material; that is, it may be included on an exam. Familiarizing yourself with the material before you hear the lecture can help you determine what is important.

2. Pay attention to what the instructor emphasizes both verbally and nonverbally.

Most professors either consciously or unconsciously emphasize important points in the material. Such an emphasis can be placed in a number of ways, one of which is voice inflection. Unless the instructor possesses an unchanging monotone, his or her voice will change when making an important point. Pitch may rise, volume may increase, speed may decrease, or any combination of these effects. Learn the meaning of the instructor's changes in voice inflection. Another way important points are emphasized is through facial expressions and body movements — particularly hand and arm movements. An intense facial expression or hand or arm movements made in conjunction with the content can help you identify important material.

The instructor may be verbally direct in placing emphasis on the important material with statements such as, "Now, this is important," or "You should know this," or "Make sure you get this down," or "You will need this later in the course." Such statements should alert you to use your best listening and recording skills because you have probably just heard a test question. If you constantly miss this clear identification of important material, you will probably have difficulty on exams.

· · · · · · · · ·

MISCONCEPTION 2:

Outlining is the most effective method of taking notes.

· · · · · · · · ·

Outlining is certainly an effective method if (1) you are good at it, (2) you think in an outline manner, and (3) your instructor presents material in an outline form. Some students simply do not think in the logical, organized manner necessary to produce an outline from material they absorb by listening. Not only must you identify the points and subpoints as these are presented, you must also be ready with the appropriate labeling. Unless the instructor says, "This is a major point," and "Here are the four subpoints," it is unlikely that you can make the major/minor decision on the spot, especially if the material is unfamiliar. Many college instructors do follow an outline of some sort when lecturing. Even so, however, it does not mean this outline will be intelligible to you as you listen. Furthermore, lectures that aren't presented from an outline are almost impossible to take outline-style notes from.

If the professor seems highly organized, you can certainly give outlined notetaking a try. Obviously some students think in the logical, systematic and organized fashion needed to outline, and for them outlining may be easy and productive. Decide which category appeals to you.

• • • • • • • • •

MISCONCEPTION 3:

Notetaking interferes with listening.
Good listening ought to be enough.

• • • • • • • • •

It is certainly true that notetaking can interfere with listening if you use inappropriate notetaking techniques. As indicated earlier, however, very few persons remember enough material just by listening to perform well on an exam. If you could be tested on the material a few hours or even a day or two after hearing it, you might pass, but unfortunately this is rarely the case. Even if you could remember material long enough to perform satisfactorily on an exam, you are only meeting a short-range objective — passing a test. You must still deal with the final exam. Remember also that that material may be related to a job you will hold after completing college. Your listening memory needs reinforcement with good notetaking.

• • • • • • • • •

MISCONCEPTION 4:

Lecture material will be covered in the text anyway, so why take notes?

• • • • • • • • •

This may be true for high school but rarely for college classes. Few professors base their lectures entirely on the assigned text; some hardly ever refer to the text. If you find an instructor who bases lectures entirely on the text, you will have a decided advantage because you will have double expo-sure to the material. You will also have the advantage of both visual and auditory stimulation. If your professor lectures directly from the text, take your copy to class and, using a yellow hi-liter, underline what the professor covers. Most professors bring in material from other books, particularly from detailed treatments of the topic and from their own research. Professors are usually scholars in their field of teaching and can supplement the text material from personal experience or a colleague's research. For example, one of the authors of this book has done research on characteristics of gifted students and is able to relate personal insights and examples in lectures related to that topic. Such additions, which usually help enrich the topic for students, are not material found in the text. So if you think that most professors cover only what is printed in the text — no more, no less — banish that thought or after an exam or two you may have some poor scores.

Obviously we have only treated a few of the more important misconceptions about the task of notetaking; others exist. The important factor for you as student is to seek out and identify the process or procedure that works for you — that helps you hear and note the important elements of the lectures you attend.

GENERAL TIPS FOR NOTETAKING

We gave a few tips on effective notetaking in the section on misconceptions. A number of other general suggestions need to be covered, however. Because listening and notetaking go hand in hand, Chapter 4 on listening is extremely important to effective notetaking, as mentioned. We also suggested that you read all assigned material before attending class. Your mental set and the knowledge gained from reading the material in advance can greatly improve your understanding and thus your notetaking. The following are additional ways to improve notetaking. Please note that these tips are related to taking notes from lectures. Notes on reading will be treated later.

1. Notes are developed rather than taken.

Taking down everything in the instructor's words, even if this were possible, is not necessarily a good technique. The words, phrases, and sentences the instructor uses belong to the instructor, not to you. Try to put the instructor's meaning in your own words — words that will have meaning for you later when you review for an exam. It is important, however, not to alter the meaning in such a way that you end up with incorrect information. Avoid changing technical terms or phrases that are fundamentally related to the understanding of the material. Sometimes words have a specialized meaning in a given context; to substitute a more common word may not reflect the meaning intended. As a general rule, however, translate the instructor's language into words you understand. It may be wise to record verbatim those statements that are technical or contain material that seems important and rephrase the statements later if appropriate. Think about how much easier it is to translate material into your own words if you are familiar with the material before the lecture.

2. Develop your vocabulary.

A large vocabulary is extremely important to your success in college because it bears on the three skills of reading, listening, and notetaking. It is difficult to extract meaning from lecture material if you do not understand either the technical or the nontechnical terms. In reading, even though it slows you and can interfere with your concentration, you have the opportunity to look up words. During a lecture, discussion, or a conversation it is virtually impossible to use a dictionary to find out the meaning of terms you don't know. It is also difficult to translate a speaker's statements into your own terms if a small vocabulary limits your understanding of the context. For example, if your American history instructor uses the term *eminent domain* but does not define it, and you have forgotten the meaning of the term, what happens to your flow of thought and concentration? There you sit wondering what *eminent domain* means; as you concentrate on it for a few seconds, the instructor moves on to other information you miss. Had you known the meaning of the term, you might not have missed what followed.

Because a good vocabulary is vital to understanding lecture material and thus to effective notetaking, you should strive to improve your vocabulary if you feel a weakness in that area. First you must verify a suspected weakness. Check the vocabulary words at the ends of chapters and the glossary in your textbooks to determine if you have vocabulary problems. Second, check old exams, if available, to determine the terms you may be expected to know. You could also take a vocabulary test to see how you measure up against other students at your level. If, after assessing yourself in terms of vocabulary, you find some gaps, you have a number of options available.

1. Develop your own vocabulary improvement program.
2. Talk with someone who teaches vocabulary development for advice.
3. Enroll in a study skills or vocabulary development short course.

The key to good vocabulary development and maintenance is to use your vocabulary. Learn the meaning of a word and then try to use it a few times during the next two or three days. If possible, use it in conversations or class discussion. If that is not possible, simply think about the word's meaning.

3. Listen carefully for summary statements.

Good instructors often summarize the major points of their lecture. Some may summarize at the end; others may make a brief summary two or three times during a lecture. It is imperative that you accurately record summary statements whenever they are made. In making summary statements, the instructor is actually giving you the lecture in capsule form. These statements are often principles, concepts, or general ideas that help you know and understand the related facts. Memorizing a few summary statements is probably not enough to ensure your mastery of a subject, but studying the material related to them should enhance your performance.

4. Connect lecture material with what you already know.

Connecting the lecture material with what you already know should enhance your learning in at least two ways. First, it should come as a boost to your self-confidence when you realize that you already know something about the material being presented. Second, it is easier to take notes when you already know something about the material; all you may need to do in such situations is jot down a few key words. Always look for associations. If you associate new material with known material, the association helps the new material become firmly entrenched in your brain.

5. Make your own diagrams or illustrations.

This is another way of translating course material into your own words. Any time you can convert a bit of content into a diagram or an illustration, it will help you to understand and remember the material. Some instructors use diagrams or other types of illustrations to represent material in a graphic manner, and you should note those as used because graphics are often helpful in recalling content. As we have seen, some students find it easier to picture a diagram or illustration than to remember words. Try to picture what is being said; if some type of graphic illustration comes to mind, jot it down. Let's use two simple diagrams as an example.

1. Suppose you wanted to picture the effect of rising oil prices on the investment in exploration. You might draw a simple graph like this:

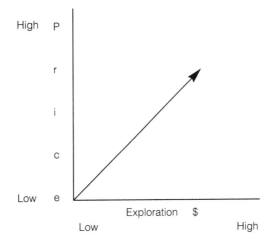

Given this illustration, you should remember that as the price of oil increases, so do efforts to find more oil.

2. Suppose you wanted to remember the three classes of levers. Using W for resistance, F for force, and Δ for fulcrum, you could diagram that information as follows:

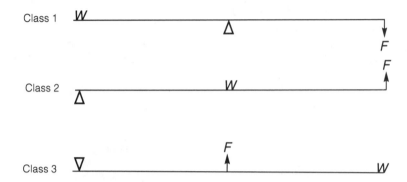

If you can make your own illustrations, it indicates that you understand the material. Another way you can put your notes in a different format is to use a flowchart. If your instructor is presenting material with related points presented in a sequence, you could build a flowchart. Put the key words of the major points in boxes and connect to other boxes which contain related points. The following simple flowchart shows the steps in sequence for preparing a speech.

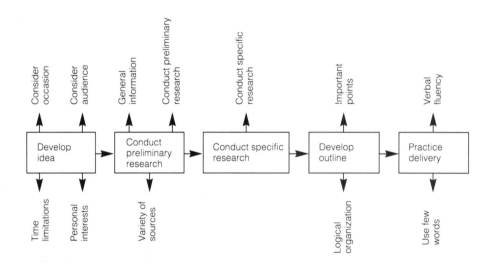

6. Use abbreviations whenever possible.

When you want to record one or more statements verbatim from the lecture, the use of abbreviations can be extremely helpful. There are, of course, some standard abbreviations you can use. For example, you do not need to spell out the name of any state because the postal service has provided standard two-letter abbreviations for all the states. Many scientific terms have abbreviations that you should use; for example, all the chemical elements have standard notations such as AU for gold, Fe for iron, and O for oxygen. Knowing these standard notations or abbreviations can help you take more complete notes in less time. Additionally, almost any word can be abbreviated, but the problem is knowing what the abbreviations mean when you review your notes. For example, you might use "prob" in your notes to stand for problem. When you review the notes, however, you can't remember if the abbreviation is for *problem* or *probably* or *probable* or *probation*. In most cases you can determine the word from the context, but you may get fooled a few times, so be careful in your use of nonstandard abbreviations.

It may be useful for you to make up your own abbreviations for words because you may remember them more easily. You can do this in two ways. (1) You can develop a common list of abbreviations from a list of most frequently used words, or from words you hear on a regular basis in classes. (2) You can also make up abbreviations as you take notes. After each abbreviation, leave some space so you can write in the full word at the end of the class or the end of the day. Writing in the full word will help avoid the problem of forgetting what the abbreviation represented.

7. Ask questions when you don't understand something.

Some students find it embarrassing to ask an instructor for clarification of a point or simply to say, "I don't understand." Probably the most common thought accompanying the question is, "I must be the only one who doesn't understand." *Rest assured you are not.* If you don't understand, others probably don't either. Many instructors try to pay attention to the attending behavior of students and make note of puzzled looks and shrugs of the shoulders. At this point they will say, "I don't think everybody got that. Let me try again," indicating that they understand the difficulty some students have in asking questions. You should not hesitate to ask a legitimate question, however. If you are hopelessly confused and don't think you can figure it out on your own later, ask. You have paid for that privilege. Sometimes it's difficult to ask questions in a large lecture (300 – 400 students) and in such situations questions are sometimes not encouraged by professors. Professors often feel that a certain amount of content must be covered and that responding to students' questions can create a time restriction. Therefore, you may want to exercise sound judgment in asking questions in both large and small classes. If you can find the material you don't understand in the text or figure it out for yourself, clarification during class may not be critical. You will also retain knowledge better if you have to hunt for it.

If the class has a laboratory section, you can often hold your questions and ask them in this smaller session. Part of the purpose of a lab section is to increase and enhance your understanding of the material. Some instructors hold help sessions that should provide you with an opportunity to have material you don't understand clarified.

8. Note principles and concepts.

Principles or concepts may contain the basic meaning you need to grasp from the lecture. Principles or concepts usually arise from or govern sets of specific facts. It is important that you record both the principle or concept and the facts if possible. This method of notetaking, called the *fact-principle system,* has the advantage of allowing you to record facts and principles at the same time and keep them in a close physical relationship. The fact-principle notetaking system works this way: Make two columns on your paper, either two equal columns or one-third and two-thirds. How you divide the page depends on the nature of the content or the ratio of facts to principles. In one column, list the facts provided in the lecture. In the other column, list the principles. You may want to put the principles on the left side, assigning a letter (A, B, C, etc.) to each one, and put the associated facts on the right side, assigning the appropriate letter and a number (A-1, A-2, etc.) to the facts, as in the examples shown here. However you do it, devise a way to associate principles with appropriate facts. If nothing else, this method will help you identify how your instructor functions. If you end up with many facts and few or no principles, you can bet your tests will be strongly factual. If you note many principles, however, the instructor may be likely to test you with essay questions.

When you prepare for a test, using notes made in this way, read through your facts and then the associated principles. Do this several times. Then read only one column and try to recall what is in the other, and vice versa. This method prepares you for an objective fact-oriented test or an essay that could be a combination of facts and principles.

Obviously the content of all classes is not appropriate for fact-principle notetaking. Try to determine your instructor's orientation by the first two meetings. If he or she functions in a manner appropriate to the fact-principle method, try it. If not, use another approach.

9. Make notes on your notes.

For various reasons you may want to make notes on your notes. This may sound like double-talk but perhaps it will make sense to you. Making notes on your notes is simply a way of condensing your class notes into a key word, idea or principle format. Why would this process be helpful? If you take copious notes, you probably need a method of shortening those notes to pull out the

· · · · · · · · · · · · · · · · · · ·

Fact-Principle Notetaking System

Economics 101
Inflation   Feb. 25, 1988

Principles	Facts
	1. economic decisions become increasingly difficult.
	2. as inflation increases there is more speculation in the purchase of goods and services.
A. Inflation has an effect on everyone	3. individuals are pushed into higher tax brackets
	4. individuals tend to shorten the planned time for the purchase of items
	1. prices rise differentially during periods of inflation
	2. all individuals do not suffer equally from inflation
B. Inflation affects prices, income and net worth	3. inflation reduces the value of savings
	4. the real value of real estate usually increases during inflation
	5. inflation causes the buyer to appear to be paying more and the seller to be receiving more.

Study Skills 101 – Oct 12, 1987
Topic – Causes of Forgetting

Most common cause of forgetting is some type of stimulus interference. This is when one stimulus interferes with another – either because they are alike or because of the time relationship. One type of forgetting is called RETROACTIVE INHIBITION, when material which is learned _after_ related material interferes. Because the stimuli are alike, the second interferes with the first.

STIMULUS INTERFERENCE

Retroactive Inhibition – later interferes with earlier

Some people believe that reading or studying just before going to bed will help reduce retroactive inhibition – there's less possibility of stimulus interference while sleeping. This may be real good for early morning exams – maybe not as good for exams later in the day.

RETROACTIVE INHIBITION

Study before sleep to reduce interference good exam prep.

Another type of interference is PROACTIVE INHIBITION. This time _earlier_ learned material interferes with later learned material

PROACTIVE INHIBITION

earlier interferes with later

Forgetting can be caused in a number of other ways. One is poor concentration when material is read or heard. We let our minds wander and read words instead of reading meaning. Sometimes reading a ¶ or two and then trying to remember what was read will help concentration. You can also try relaxing before reading or before going to class.

Another cause – INFORMATION OVERLOAD – too much information in too short a time. This can make it hard to sort out all the information. Help? – Spacing study over longer periods of time can help. Not waiting til the day before the exam also helps.

Forgetting may be related to one big question – DID I REALLY LEARN? When does a person know when material really was learned? Simply reading material or listening in class does not necessarily mean material was learned.

To really learn, you must read and recall a number of times. This seems to be best way to retain information properly

Forgetting Other Causes

poor concentration

distractions

read-remember

relax

INFORMATION Overload

space study

no all-nighters

WAS MATERIAL LEARNED?

reading and listening not enough

READ AND RECALL

key elements. Using this process, while your notes are fresh, will also give you a chance to verify what you wrote and provide your first review of the material. When you are studying for an exam you can study both the key elements and the lengthier notes.

To implement this strategy, you need to leave about one-fourth to one-third of the page blank. Use the larger portion for making notes in class and leave the small portion for making notes on your notes after class or later on that same day. The example below should give you an idea of how this system works.

10. Label and organize your notes.

Attention to the following simple details can greatly improve your notes' usability.

1. Keep notes for each class in a separate notebook or in separate sections of a tabbed looseleaf notebook.
2. Label notes from each class session by course and topic.
3. Number the pages.
4. Date each page of your notes.
5. Leave wide margins or vertical spacing for details on the notes you will add later from the course text.

NOTETAKING ON BOOKS

Notetaking from your assigned text is usually as important as notetaking from lectures. Though the purpose of both is essentially the same, the process involved is a bit different. Good notes on lectures are a function of listening and recording skills; good notes on textbooks are a function of reading skill. Studying Chapter 6 should help you take better notes. Other suggestions follow.

1. Use a hi-lite pen.

If the book belongs to you, use a pastel hi-liter to mark important material. You must be selective in choosing what you hi-lite. Don't mark too much, but what *is* too much? That's a good question. The amount you hi-lite depends on a number of factors. How does the author organize the material? Do the major points and subpoints stand out clearly? Is every page packed with principles and supporting facts? If, for example, the material is presented as major points and subpoints, it should be fairly obvious what to hi-lite. If, on the other hand, the author writes in a rambling disconnected style, deciding what to hi-lite will be much more difficult. You must simply become familiar with the author's style. As a general rule, you will probably hi-lite about one-fourth or less of the material on a page, but understand that this amount will vary with each page and subject.

You may want to distinguish between the major and minor points that you hi-lite. Perhaps putting an asterisk beside the major points will help them stand out. Remember, major points are often repeated more than once in a text and may also be mentioned by your instructor.

Try to isolate and hi-lite principles and generalizations and the specific facts associated with them. Use lines and arrows to physically relate the facts to the principles or letter the principle and number its associated facts, as in fact-principle notetaking. However you do it, hi-lite these principles and generalizations because they will be the foundation for exams.

2. Jot down important points.

Some students may not want to hi-lite material in their books because they remember material better if they make notes while reading. If you want to take notes as you read, consider some organized method of doing this. Remember, you want to make these notes useful to you at a later time. You may simply want to number each major point and then list subpoints, or you may choose to use a modified outline form. Leave space in the margins to add material or make notes on your notes: Suppose, for example, your instructor indicates in class that something mentioned in the text is very important. Go back to your text notes or the text and write *This is important* next to that point.

Remember that simply using this method, as well as the hi-liter technique, does not necessarily mean you *understand* the material. You may simply be hi-liting sentences or writing words on your paper. Think about the importance of reading the material carefully before you hi-lite or take notes.

3. Use the précis method.

A *précis* is a concise abridgement or summary. Making summary statements after reading a given amount of material can be an effective notetaking method as well as a helpful study tool. To make an accurate summary statement in your own words, you will need to use the skill of synthesizing mentioned in Chapter 6. You are condensing large amounts of material into a few statements, and to do this you must understand the material. If you stumble around or are puzzled about what to write, this may be a good indication that you do not understand the material. Later, when reviewing for a quiz or a test, go over the summary statements and determine if you know the material associated with the statements.

Because you are making summary statements, you are probably not recording facts. If you are the type of learner who can remember the facts associated with the broad statements, the précis method could be useful. If you feel more comfortable recording facts, however, you would need to alter the précis method to include facts.

4. Outline the material.

Outlining is a useful method for taking notes on written material if certain conditions are present. First, the written material must be organized and presented in such a way that it is outlineable. Second, you must have the skill to identify the main point and subpoints and condense these into terse, abbreviated statements. Third, you must have the right attitude toward outlining. Outlining is difficult for some people because they don't think in the appropriate manner to outline properly.

Once you have decided that you can mentally handle the outline format, consider the way the book is organized. Has the author used main headings and one, two, or three subheadings? Do major points fall under the main headings and subpoints and specific facts under the subheadings? Are the points clear and succinct rather than disguised with unnecessary rhetoric?

If, after examining the material, you are satisfied that outlining is feasible, try that approach. Use any standard outline model—the one you learned in elementary school is fine. Don't become overly concerned with symmetry. The outline is just for you; no one is going to evaluate whether it is or isn't symmetrical. Make the outline work for you; don't let it control you. Leave space in the left margin to make notes on your outline.

5. Use a tape recorder.

If you happen to be a person who learns more effectively by listening and speaking rather than by silently reading, you may want to read material into a tape recorder. Instead of reading verbatim, moreover, you may want to record summary statements of the material. For example, suppose you read the following statement into the recorder: "Biology, Chapter 5, topic, photosynthesis: 'Photosynthesis is the process of forming carbohydrates in living plants from water and carbon dioxide.' . . ." You can put numerous statements of this type on a single tape.

How much time do you spend in your automobile? If you have a cassette player in your car, you have a way of playing your tapes. You can also purchase an adaptor, which fits into the cigarette lighter, to power a portable cassette recorder. Instead of playing Michael Jackson or Huey Lewis and the News or El Debarge, put your biology or philosophy or economics tape in the cassette player. If you think about the time you spend in your car alone, you could probably gain three or four hours of additional study time per week. If you have recorded summary statements, you can probably listen to a summary of three chapters in a half hour or less.

You can also tape lectures and play the tapes over and over again. This is helpful if the lectures are dense and full of information—and if your instructor gives you permission to record. Perhaps the most effective way is to read a summary of your notes into the recorder, allowing you to eliminate the chaff, keep the wheat, and take an active part yourself in the presentation of the material.

6. Use a word processor.

Students who own or have access to a computer with a word processor can use that tool effectively for storage of lecture notes or notes from readings. All it takes to store lecture notes is to type in the notes or summaries of the notes at the end of each day. For text notes, simply type in what you have hi-lited or underlined. You can also read sections of the material and, after you understand it, feed a summary into the computer. However you choose to do it, you now have a computerized record stored and available at your request.

PUTTING YOUR LECTURE NOTES TO WORK

As soon as possible after a class session, finish your notes. You may be thinking, "What do you mean—I finished my notes when the class ended." Generally speaking, notes are not complete when you leave the class. To complete them, you must:

1. Spell out any words you have abbreviated.
2. Correctly spell words you couldn't spell during class and look up the meanings of words you don't know.
3. Hi-lite the main ideas.
4. Make notes on your notes for quick reference.
5. Read through your notes—this initial review helps implant the content in your mind.
6. As you read through your notes, recite them aloud to help you remember the content while it is fresh.

Review

Effective notetaking is an essential skill for success in college. The ability to take clear, understandable notes on lectures, textbooks, and other assigned readings can make the difference between success and failure. If you don't feel you are a good notetaker, think about your perceived purpose for notes, your style of taking notes, your listening skills, and your preparation for class.

The important points to remember about good notetaking are:

1. Notes are developed rather than taken.
2. A large vocabulary helps.

3. Using abbreviations facilitates the process.

4. Your notes aren't finished when you leave class.

5. Principles and concepts are important to record.

Review Questions

1. What are some common misconceptions about notetaking? Do you have ideas or practices related to notetaking that you should examine?

2. How does a small vocabulary interfere with your understanding and effective recording of lecture notes?

3. Do you feel your vocabulary is adequate? If not, what can you do to improve it?

4. How can graphics help you understand material better?

5. Do you normally use abbreviations? Can you develop the ability to use abbreviations?

6. Why is it helpful to understand the principles related to a course?

For Further Reading

Farquhar, William et al. *Learning to Study*. New York: R. A. Roudd Press, 1960.

Ruetten, Mark K. *Comprehending Academic Lectures*. New York: Macmillan, 1986.

Sotiriou, Peter Elias. *Interpreting College Study Skills*. Belmont, Calif.: Wadsworth, 1984.

Phipps, Rita. *The Successful Student's Handbook*. Seattle: University of Washington Press, 1983.

Gilbert, Doris Wilcox. *Study in Depth*. Englewood Cliffs, N.J.: Prentice-Hall, 1966.

Pauk, Walter. *How to Study in College*. Boston: Houghton Mifflin, 1984.

READING AS A KEY TO SUCCESS

• • • • •

Reading is one of the two most common learning modes you will use in your college career. The other is listening, which was treated in Chapter 4. To be a successful college student, you must be an effective reader, which means much more than simply reading the words on the page of a textbook. Good reading means comprehending in both a literal and inferential sense. It means grasping the details and the broad sense. It means remembering what you read. The purpose of this chapter is to help you understand the reading process better and to improve your reading habits. Specific goals are:

1. To help you internalize the importance of effective reading skills to success in college
2. To help you enhance existing reading skills
3. To help you develop new reading skills
4. To help you learn to use various reading techniques
5. To help you improve your comprehension

Unfortunately, many people do not read effectively. More unfortunately, perhaps, some of those people go to college. Unless ineffective readers find ways to improve, their chances of success are slim because almost all college courses are based strongly on reading. How do you measure up in terms of effective reading? If you are not sure, complete the following reading inventory. Respond honestly—no one but you will see this.

TRUE   FALSE

——   ——   1.   My mind frequently wanders when I read assignments.

——   ——   2.   I often need to read sentences or paragraphs two or more times to grasp their meaning.

——   ——   3.   I try to avoid difficult material.

——   ——   4.   I often do not understand words I encounter while reading.

——   ——   5.   I usually read each word and hear the word in my brain.

——   ——   6.   I have trouble deciding which facts are important.

——   ——   7.   I usually just start reading without determining the specific objectives I want to reach.

——   ——   8.   I often read surrounded by distractions, that is, in the student lounge, TV room at home, and so on.

——   ——   9.   I usually read all textbooks or library materials the same way.

_____ _____ 10. I usually do not pay much attention to charts, maps, tables, pictures, diagrams, and graphs when I am reading.

_____ _____ 11. I rarely read the questions and look at vocabulary words at the end of a chapter before I read the chapter.

_____ _____ 12. I usually just start reading rather than first looking over a chapter to see how it is organized.

_____ _____ 13. I usually don't try to relate reading material to my personal experience or what I already know.

_____ _____ 14. I have little confidence in my ability to read and remember.

If you answered "true" to more than half these questions, you may lack some reading skill and/or approach the task of reading in an inappropriate manner. Obviously this survey was not scientifically developed, but it does point to some important elements related to effective reading.

Although a few techniques exist that help students become more effective readers, there are really no shortcuts. The most effective path to success in reading, and in college, is hard work, which is even harder if you do not possess adequate reading skills. Studying the material and applying the ideas in this chapter can reduce the hard work, but even effective readers spend a great deal of time reading textbooks. To be a successful college student, therefore, you must make a commitment to spend a great deal of time reading.

MENTALLY PREPARING FOR READING

Two mental factors are involved in effective reading. These, not in any order of importance, are:

Motivation

If your only reason for reading a chapter in the text or reading library material is to meet an instructor's requirements, you may lack the necessary or appropriate motivation. You may view the instructor's requirements as external or extrinsic rather than internal or intrinsic. Remember, you are not completing an assignment or reading a chapter for the instructor—_you are doing it for yourself._ The instructor only provides you with input and reading material that he/she feels will help you learn the content of the course. In every course you take, you also need to accept the instructor's requirements _as your requirements and your responsibility_ whether you do or don't agree with them.

Think of your long-range goal, which for most college students is to be gainfully employed in the field of speciality indicated by their degree. A shorter-range goal within the long-range goal is to obtain the degree. Obviously, the short-range goal of getting the degree demands the successful completion of courses. Therefore, what you do in courses to meet requirements helps you achieve that long-range goal. If you have difficulty getting motivated to read, think of those long-range goals. Sometimes students have more difficulty becoming motivated to read for elective or general education courses: "I am majoring in marketing," runs this thinking, "so why do I have to take a course in English literature? I don't care what Shakespeare wrote." Why are such courses required of a marketing or math or chemistry major? One reason is that general education courses provide you with a broad educational background as your major gives you in-depth education. General education courses provide the content needed to consider a person educated rather than trained. Try to remember this if you have difficulty keeping your motivation up for reading in those general education courses.

Concentration

Do you sometimes find your mind wandering as you try to concentrate on reading a text or a journal article? Do you reread a sentence or a paragraph two or three times before you know what it says? Do you stop in the middle, ask yourself what you just read, and find that you don't know? These conditions could indicate lack of concentration, lack of understanding, or both. Let us assume for the moment that lack of concentration is the problem. Poor concentration can be caused by any one of a number of reasons. Some of those reasons and ways of dealing with them follow.

• • • • • • • • • •

A CLEAR PURPOSE CAN LEAD TO IMPROVED CONCENTRATION

• • • • • • • • • •

Lack of a goal or purpose can lead to poor concentration. Know why you are reading and what you want to get from the material.

• • • • • • • • • •

IMPROVED VOCABULARY CAN LEAD TO IMPROVED CONCENTRATION

• • • • • • • • • •

Too many unknown words can affect your concentration, partly because it is irritating not to know the meaning of words, but they also interfere with your rhythm and tempo. Find the meaning of words you don't know—then read for understanding.

• • • • • • • • • •

CLEARING YOUR MIND OF EXTRANEOUS THOUGHTS CAN LEAD TO IMPROVED CONCENTRATION

• • • • • • • • • •

Too many extraneous thoughts running through your brain can definitely interfere with your concentration. Such extraneous thoughts can be random and relatively unimportant, or they can relate to serious problems. If your thoughts are reminiscences about events of the past few hours or about non-serious events of the next few hours, it may help to put the book down, close your eyes, and let those thoughts flow for a few minutes. Whatever strategy you use, you must put those extraneous thoughts out of your mind.

If, on the other hand, they concern serious problems, stop reading and concentrate on your problem. Try mentally to make progress toward a solution. Feeling as if you have a handle on a solution may lessen your concern. If you cannot remove those problem thoughts, put the book down because you are probably wasting time. If your inability to remove problems from your mind while you are trying to concentrate on other matters persists, you may want to discuss this with someone. In most cases, counselors are available on campus to help you with such problems.

• • • • • • • • • •

OVERCOMING OR AVOIDING DISTRACTIONS CAN LEAD TO IMPROVED CONCENTRATION

• • • • • • • • • •

Auditory and/or visual interferences are common causes of poor concentration. Some persons are distracted by auditory stimuli, others are distracted by visual stimuli. What sorts of things distract you while you attempt to read and concentrate? Are they primarily auditory or visual? Auditory distractions can be persons talking too loud at another table in the library, footsteps, television, loud music, machinery operating near your study area, or any one of a number of noises. Visual distractions can be someone working, people moving about, an attractive member of the opposite sex nearby, mental images, or various other things you see. Usually you can control these distractions simply by moving to another location where they are not present. You can almost always find an acceptable study area if you look around.

There is little point in continuing to list possible interferences. You should know yourself well enough to figure out what interferes with your concentration. The following are three ideas that could help you improve concentration for reading and study.

1. *Relax before you read.* Assume a comfortable position, close your eyes

and think of a pleasant event, place, or setting. Fix this picture in your mind and let the pleasant thoughts flow. A number of relaxation exercises are available on audio tape cassettes that can be purchased at a reasonable price. Generally, people concentrate more effectively if they can relax and reduce some of their tensions.

2. *Listen to music while you read.* Contrary to what you may believe, rock music may hinder rather than aid concentration. Through experiments with different types of music, researchers have found that baroque music seems to assist concentration (Ostrander & Schroeder, 1979). Try listening to the music of Bach, Handel, or Corelli instead of Sting.

3. *Use deep breathing exercises for a few minutes before you read.* Assume a comfortable position and relax your entire body. Close your eyes and breathe deeply and slowly through your nose. Take in as much air as you can hold. Exhale slowly and try to force all the air out of your lungs. Do this a few times and then try to breathe in rhythm. Inhale to a count of four, hold to a count of four, exhale to a count of four, and pause to a count of four. Do this a few times, then increase the count to six and then to eight. Such rhythmic breathing will help synchronize body and mind functions (Ostrander & Schroeder, 1979).

READING WITH A PURPOSE

Perhaps the first factor about reading you need to internalize is that there are different types of reading. You may not have learned to read in different ways during elementary or secondary school. If you have not had this training, it would be to your advantage to mentally accept different approaches to reading and then implement those approaches. Some people have a mental block about reading textbooks in any way other than word for word. Reading a textbook means reading carefully because one will be held accountable for the material. Careful reading, they think, is reading word for word. This attitude is one you may want to reconsider. Good reading is not always verbatim reading.

You will find some different approaches to reading treated in this section. *Surveying* is a technique for achieving an overview of the material. *Rapid reading* is a technique for moving quickly through material. *Reading for thorough comprehension* is simply reading for understanding and remembering. We will consider each of these techniques in turn.

Surveying

Use surveying when you want a quick overview of a book or when you are searching for some piece of information you will recognize on sight. Before you begin to read a text, take fifteen to twenty minutes to familiarize yourself with the format and contents of the book. During this overview you could look for the following.

1. How are the chapters organized?

Obviously, authors arrange their chapters in different ways, but common elements are usually present. Some books contain objectives or a preview at the beginning that will give you an outline of the important elements in each chapter. Almost always chapters have major subheadings that relate directly to the chapter title. The subheadings often contain different aspects of the main topic for example, a controversial aspect of the main topic under which there are three or more theories or viewpoints. These theories or viewpoints could be treated as minor subheadings. Divisions (major and minor subheadings) within a chapter can be developed in a number of ways. Sometimes the development depends on the nature of the content. A history text is usually organized chronologically, but the chapters could focus on major events within the given span of time. Science and math texts are almost always organized from the simplest to the most complex material in that subject, and the relationship of the topics is systematic. A management text may be organized in terms of major strategies or themes related to effective management. An art or literature text may be organized by types. However the text is organized, study the pattern and pay attention to divisions within chapters. Pay especially careful attention to major and minor subheadings because they will identify the main content.

2. What learning aids are contained at the ends of chapters and at the end of the book?

Look at the ends of the chapters. Is there a summary? Are there review questions? Is there a glossary of terms? Check the end of the book for a glossary. Are there appendices? Often these will contain detailed statistical data, charts, tables, graphs, and the like. These are all valuable aids for effective learning. If they exist, *use* them.

3. Does the book contain charts, graphs, tables, diagrams, maps, or other graphics?

Information displayed in graphic form is often easier to absorb than the same material put into words. The heavy use of graphics could indicate an emphasis on facts or the relationships among factual or statistical data.

4. What are the book's physical features?

Is the print small or large? Does the book seem crowded, that is, with little space between the lines? Do the subheadings stand out? These are all physical features that may affect your mindset and hence your desire to read.

5. Are key words or phrases emphasized?

Does the author identify important words or phrases with italics or bold type? If so, you have been provided with a valuable learning aid.

Besides previewing, another use of the surveying technique of reading is to search for particular material. Often you will need to look quickly through a textbook or a reference book to locate certain material. If you are doing a term paper or project, you can survey a number of possible source books rapidly to find what you need. First, check the table of contents to determine if the book contains relevant material. If it does, survey the interior for the material you need.

Rapid Reading

Rapid reading is a technique for moving quickly through material. Unlike surveying, however, the purpose of rapid reading is not to find isolated bits of information but to read and retain actual *content*. There are, of course, many kinds of rapid reading techniques, a few of which will be presented here.

Perhaps the most important factor related to rapid reading is your attitude about reading. To read rapidly and effectively, you must overcome the read-every-word syndrome. It is simply not necessary that you read every word in a paragraph to extract the meaning. The problem with reading every word is that you may be reading words rather than meaning. The structure of language is such that the meaning is contained in combinations of words or phrases, clauses, and sentences. Reading one word after another often results in a lower level of understanding than reading the meaning contained in phrases and clauses.

Besides working to make your attitude about reading more flexible, you must also learn to develop faster eye movements. Try to avoid letting your eyes stop to focus on each word. One of the keys to good rapid reading is to keep your eyes moving. Using nonessential material such as a newspaper, practice moving your eyes rapidly across a line of print. Don't worry about retention at this point. Try a few lines — stop, look away — and see if you recall anything from the material. You may be surprised at how much you have absorbed in this manner. It really isn't amazing because you are reading even if you aren't pronouncing or sounding every word. Your eyes act like a camera lens and send the meaning in the printed material directly to your brain.

Another rapid reading method is to move your eyes from top to bottom down the page. This is more difficult with wide columns so you should develop the technique on narrow-columned material such as newspapers or magazines. Practice the same way you would in moving your eyes rapidly from left to right but now move your eyes *down* the page. Practice with nonessential material, moving your eyes 3 or 4 inches down the column. Stop, look away, and determine if you absorbed anything. As with left-to-right rapid reading, your mind will absorb the essential material without your reading every word. You pick up words with your peripheral vision without realizing it.

You can practice increasing the speed of your eye movements and widening your peripheral vision in a number of ways. One way is to use a *tachisto-scope,* a machine in which material is flashed on a screen so rapidly that you do not have time to read every word and are thus forced to let your eyes function as a camera. This is a frustrating experience at first, but with effort you will learn the technique. You may want to enroll in a speed reading course, which should be available on your campus or in the night school of a local high school. It is not unusual for individuals to double or triple their reading speed through rapid reading courses. Even if you don't quite have the faith to use rapid reading with essential material, use it for reading nonessential material and save time that way.

Short of formal means, you can practice rapid reading techniques in other ways. Try glancing quickly (a fraction of a second) at signs, billboards, car license plates, names on trucks or businesses, and the like, avoiding actually reading the words or numbers. Then try to recall what you read, words or numbers. Practice as often as you can and you will probably be surprised by how much your reading speed will increase.

When Is Rapid Reading Appropriate?   Rapid reading is an appropriate technique for a number of reading purposes. Use rapid reading as:

1. A way to preread before reading for thorough comprehension.
2. A way to pull out the main ideas from a chapter or chapter section.
3. A way to search for particular details related to an idea or principle.
4. A way to respond to a set of study questions related to an exam.
5. A way to review for an exam. (Rapid reading is helpful as a review if you are familiar with the material or if you have hi-lited important parts.)

READING FOR THOROUGH COMPREHENSION

You have already read the sections on surveying and rapid reading — techniques to help you become familiar with a printed work and to move through material rapidly. These reading techniques can also be considered *prereading* for thorough understanding. Reading for thorough comprehension should be used when you:

1. Want to remember the material for a later purpose — another course or a test.
2. Want to absorb the full flavor of the material, as when reading a novel.
3. Feel the author packs each sentence and paragraph with useful information.
4. Know the material is essential to understanding your major area of study.

Types of Comprehension

To know what is meant by *reading comprehension*, you must realize that different types of comprehension exist.

Although reading experts will classify comprehension in different ways, there are essentially two levels of comprehension — literal and inferential. *Literal comprehension* is understanding the specific or exact meaning of the information. In other words one does not have to interpret — only retell what one knows. *Inferential comprehension* is understanding information in terms of what the information might mean. A few lines from Shakespeare's *Julius Caesar* may help clarify the difference between literal and inferential comprehension.

> Let me have men about me that are fat;
>
> Sleek-headed men and such as sleep o' nights;
>
> Yond Cassius has a lean and hungry look;
>
> He thinks too much: Such men are dangerous.

Literally, Caesar's words "lean and hungry" — mean that Cassius did not get enough to eat and couldn't sleep at night. Inferentially, Caesar is saying that Cassius spends his time thinking and plotting. Men who do such things look lean and hungry; that is, they are not satisfied with conditions and want change. To understand inferentially, you must interpret the information rather than accept its literal meaning. Inferential comprehension includes reasoning; understanding implications, judgments, applications; and understanding inferences. Notice that these functions involve higher levels of thinking than recall and retelling, which are associated with literal comprehension.

Inferential comprehension can be divided into a number of categories or subsections. As a way of understanding these levels of understanding, it may be useful to look at levels of learning or thinking and relate the two. Benjamin Bloom (1956) suggested that six levels of cognitive learning existed:

```
                                                    Evaluation
                                                       :
                                      Synthesis        :
                                         :
                        Analysis         :
                           :
          Application      :
             :
Comprehension :
   :
Cognitive :
Memory   :
```

Bloom's levels of thinking are depicted here as stairs to indicate a hierarchy, ranging from cognitive memory at the lowest level to evaluation at the highest level. They may be defined as follows:

1. *Cognitive memory* is the recall or recognition of information: what, where, when, or who.

2. *Comprehension* is the level of learning that shows understanding of the information one possesses, as demonstrated through description, explanation, personal definition, or translations into one's own words.

3. *Application* is the level of learning involved in the transfer of knowledge. One can recall information and explain it, but this level deals with applying the information to another situation, that is, problem solving. In solving an algebra equation, for example, you must apply your knowledge of solving equations to a specific equation.

4. *Analysis* is the level of learning involved in examining component parts of something as an idea or theory. When you isolate the facts or ideas that make up a concept, generalization, or theory, you are analyzing. In other words, analysis is identification of the parts that make up the whole.

5. *Synthesis* is the level of learning involved in making something out of the component parts: If a professor gives you four related facts and asks that you develop a theory or generalization, synthesis is being used. Creating new information based on facts is another example.

6. *Evaluation* is the level of learning used when one applies criteria to determine the worth or value of an idea, a function, or a thing. The criteria or standards can be external or internal to the individual doing evaluative thinking.

Relating Bloom's Taxonomy, as it is known, to literal and inferential comprehension, literal comprehension would include cognitive memory and comprehension and inferential comprehension would include application, analysis, synthesis, and evaluation. These levels of learning will be treated further later.

It is important to understand *comprehension* as something more complex than a single state of mind. If you can see your comprehension taking place at various *levels*, this can influence the way you read. Ineffective readers generally read all material the same way, which is usually reading only for the specifics or literal meaning. The effective reader, on the other hand, considers the meaning of the material while reading it; he or she is comprehending at a higher level than the literal. The student who walks into an exam loaded with facts to feed back to the instructor and finds that exam questions deal with an interpretation of factual material will probably have some difficulty with the exam.

Literal Comprehension

The purpose of literal comprehension is to grasp the direct or exact meaning and to obtain the specific fact or ideas as presented. Cognitive memory and comprehension are the learning levels usually involved in the understanding and retention of ideas and facts. Learning at those levels is very important because it is difficult to learn at higher levels (analysis, synthesis, evaluation) unless your comprehension is already complete at the lower levels of learning. Specific reading skills or reader functions associated with literal comprehension are:

1. Understanding the exact meaning of terms, especially discipline-specific or technical terms.

2. Understanding the meaning of facts or principles as stated. After reading a sentence or paragraph that contains a fact or principle, stop and think about what you have read. Do you understand the material? How does it fit with other data you have already read?

3. Following exact directions when the author suggests that you think through a process or asks you to perform some function with paper and pencil. Usually what you are asked to do is a proven process that the author feels will help you understand or remember the fact or idea.

4. Responding to the review questions at the end of the chapter after reading the material. Note those that call for literal understanding of the material. What are the facts, ideas, or principles the author has chosen to use in review questions? Not only will answering these questions help you decide if you remembered anything, the questions themselves will serve as a guide to what the author considers important.

5. Studying the material in graphs, tables, and other visuals because these are valuable sources of information to help you understand content. Especially when you are reading for facts, do not skip over the graphics.

A significant part of the reading you do in college will be for the purpose of developing a *factual base* and recalling that information for future use. A factual base could be interpreted in a number of ways. It could mean that the knowledge base you develop will help you to be culturally literate. Cultural literacy simply means that you have a knowledge base beyond your major area—that you know something about culture in terms of art, literature, music, history, etc. A factual base can also be in any given subject area that makes it possible for you to advance in that subject, that is, to learn at higher levels. Therefore, the significant investment of time you make in reading for literal comprehension will not be wasted.

Inferential Comprehension

Inferential comprehension is understanding well enough so that you can apply, analyze, synthesize or evaluate the material. Obviously the ability to interpret or infer requires an understanding of the material in a literal sense, i.e., knowing the facts. As you read for literal understanding, you should also think about the inferential aspect, if any, related to the material. Higher levels of learning as these apply to inferential skills are treated below.

The ability to use or apply what you have learned to a different but related situation is a demonstration of a higher level of learning. Using formulas to solve a math problem is an example of application; so is performing certain experiments in science classes. For example, the characteristics—texture, color, hardness—that distinguish sedimentary, igneous, and metamorphic rock from one another is factual data. Applying your literal knowledge of those characteristics to classify a group of rocks is comprehension at the application level. Some students almost automatically read with thoughts toward how the information they are absorbing might be used, but the application possibility never occurs to others. As you read, think of how the facts could be used in a practical situation. Often your instructor will make such statements as, "You can use this when you do . . ." or "You will need this information for another course in your program." When you hear statements like this, listen selfishly and, if you don't have a good understanding of the material mentioned, probe your text, find the material, and learn it.

Reading for Exams

It is not unusual to be asked on an exam to compare or contrast two ideas; two plots in novels; two theories in sociology, psychology, or physics; two religions; or two philosophies. Such questions require you to deal with the relationship, or lack of one, between two items. Rather than waiting until you are asked to produce such data on an exam, start thinking of comparisons and contrasts as you read; quiz yourself on how two theories or two philosophical positions are alike or different. Through this process you will understand each theory better and also prepare yourself to respond to an essay question on the topic.

A second essay question type requires you to *analyze* a statement, idea, theory, or philosophical position. This type of question requires deductive thinking because you are thinking from the general to the specific—from the whole to its parts. You must know clearly what various facts and principles constitute or support the idea, theory, or position. As you read, note whether the author uses *deductive thinking* (general idea, then the facts or elements related to the idea). If a deductive approach is used, the analysis question should be easy for you to handle on an exam—if you have read the material properly. For example, suppose you were asked on a test to analyze a bull stock market. You know what a bull market is, so you identify the economic and other conditions that when present, create a bull market.

A third essay question type asks you to draw a generalization from a group of facts. This type of thinking is called *synthesis* and requires you to use *inductive thinking,* that is, from the specific (facts) to the general (a generalization, principle or idea). In other words, you are asked to determine how a group of facts can be used to form a general statement. To do this properly, you must know what is common among the facts, that is, how they relate to each other. Using the same example as earlier, suppose you were given a list of economic conditions and asked what kind of market might develop. In this case you are asked to put conditions together to form an overview, to synthesize those conditions into a whole. Again, the time to think about how facts fit together or relate is when you are reading. As with deductive thinking, note how the author develops the material. If an inductive approach (specific to general) is used, you should be able to handle that type of essay question. Some authors develop material using both inductive and deductive approaches; some do not. Therefore, if only one approach is used, try to think in the opposite manner from that used by the author.

Some specific skills or types of questions related to inferential comprehension are:

1. Summarize the major points related to . . .
2. What might have happened if . . . ?
3. In novel X, how does the author use characters, setting, and theme to develop plot?
4. Do you agree with the author's conclusions? Why or why not?
5. What was the author trying to convey with his/her writing style?
6. Which of the following are facts and which opinions? Support your answer.

The highest level of thinking in Bloom's Taxonomy and another type of inferential comprehension is evaluation, wherein the thinker evaluates or judges an idea, opinion, process, statement, or position against a standard or criterion. Obviously, value judgments are involved in evaluative thinking, but the value judgments must have a base — they should not be delivered off the top of one's head in a disorganized fashion. Sometimes the examinee may be asked to develop criteria and then evaluate the item in terms of these criteria. Evaluative thinking requires thorough understanding of the material in terms of both literal and inferential comprehension. For example, suppose you were asked to evaluate whether the author of a certain novel followed the normal pattern of development for a novel. In this case (unless the material has been provided by the instructor) you must know what that typical development pattern is, how the author developed novel X, and relate the two.

DIFFERENTIAL READING

Another way of improving your reading skill is to use a technique we will call *differential reading,* which simply means that you read material in different ways according to its content.

It is highly unlikely that your formal reading instruction in elementary or secondary school included how to read different types of content. Reading is reading, correct? No, because different subject areas require different types of thinking; therefore, it follows that different types of reading are needed. Not only does each discipline have its own jargon and technical or special language, textbooks are usually developed and organized according to the structure of their discipline. Authors of books in the hard sciences and mathematics tend toward a strong factual base with logical, systematic, sequential development; as you read a text organized in this way, you should employ your factual, logical, and systematic thinking processes. On the other hand, authors of textbooks in the humanities and social sciences tend to follow a chronological and/or thematic development. You must read chronologically organized books in a sequential manner; you must read thematically organized books in an integrative, interpretive, or idea-oriented manner. (Note, however, that some of these differences may be a function of author preference rather than subject area.)

Typically, the average college student will read books in fifteen to twenty different subject areas during four years of college. Though there is clearly overlap in reading strategies, some different approaches must be used to read effectively. It is not our intention here to describe specific strategies for all subject areas, only to provide a few suggestions.

When reading a math text, you must pay total attention to the example problems because they provide the concrete examples of the written material. It is probably wise to have pencil and paper ready to work the sample problems rather than just look at the ones in the book. If you have difficulty understanding the process, read the explanation again and try another sample problem. Success in math requires more than the ability to manipulate numbers and letters, it requires understanding of the theory and the conceptual structure of the discipline. Because mathematics functions tend to build on previous functions, it is doubly important that you understand each function as they are presented in sequence.

Hard sciences textbooks are often developed from a logical perspective, which means that the material is usually presented in some type of sequence. Because of its highly factual content, literal comprehension becomes very important, at least for your initial understanding of the content. Beginning textbooks in the hard sciences do not devote much space to speculation because the factual base must first be established. Therefore, as you read texts in the hard sciences use every skill you know to develop your factual base.

Facts are also important in reading in the social sciences, but in these fields concepts and generalizations are important early. Material may not be developed in as obvious an ordered sequence as in math or science because there may not be a natural or logical order in the material. Literal comprehension is important in the social sciences, but you must also read with inferential comprehension in mind and know the concepts and/or generalizations related to facts. Therefore, you must do a great deal of inductive thinking when reading in the social science.

In the humanities it is important to think of the implied meaning in the material. Certainly some humanities courses spin off a factual base, but interpretations and inferences made from the material are equally important, if not moreso. Much of humanities material consists of ideas or speculations by the author or significant thinkers. As in social sciences, the factual base for humanities is not as strong as in the hard sciences.

Some people like some subject areas better than others. The reasons for such preferences are probably related to the way we think. Those of us who think in a logical, rational, orderly fashion with a facility for understanding and remembering facts probably enjoy math and the hard sciences and perhaps courses such as economics or accounting. On the other hand, those of us who think interpretatively, creatively, intuitively, and holistically probably prefer the humanities and social sciences. Further, those who think technically, administratively, and financially probably prefer business courses. It can be tough if you prefer to think one way but must take courses where you are required to think in an almost opposite way. Thus it is important that you build on your strengths but also work to develop other types of thinking or functioning skills.

READING GRAPHICS

Even though we have mentioned graphics earlier, a special note here seems useful. Students often mistakenly assume that all the knowledge lies in words, but visual material must be carefully read as well. These include graphs, diagrams, tables, maps, and other visuals.

Generally, graphs are of three types: bar graphs, line graphs, and circle or pie graphs. *Bar graphs* usually compare relative amounts of two items or to indicate the distribution of two or more items. The sample bar graph here shows the growth of the consumer price index (CPI) for automobiles as compared with the consumer price index for all other items in the 1972–1980 period. Study the graph and:

1. Make two general statements about it.

2. Try to draw conclusions about why the difference in the two indices was greater in some years than others.

3. Think about what other products or services might have increased more than the CPI for all items.

• • • • • • • • • • • • • • • • • •
Consumer Price Index Against New Car Prices, 1972–1980

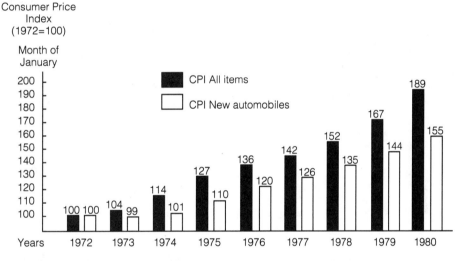

Note: All data based on historical CPI-Urban Wage Earners and Clerical Workers.
Source: U.S. Dept. of Labor, Bureau of Labor Statistics.

Circle or *pie graphs* show the distribution of an item in relation to the total quantity of that item. Amounts are expressed in percentages that should total 100 percent. The example here shows a profile of General Motors stockholders in terms of the percentage of stockholders in relation to number of shares. Study the graph and:

1. Determine the percentage of stockholders who own 100 shares or less.

2. Determine the percentage of stockholders who own 50 shares or less.

3. Draw a conclusion about GM stockholders.

4. Think about what the same graph might look like for the year 1987.

• •

GM Holders of Common Stock, By Size of Holdings.

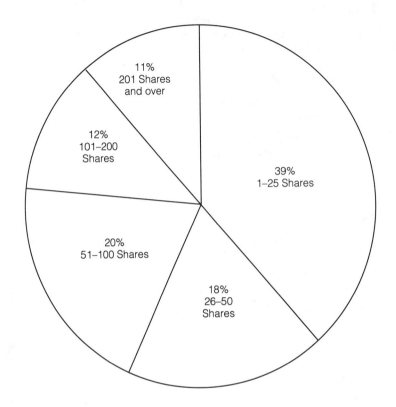

11%
201 Shares
and over

12%
101–200
Shares

39%
1–25 Shares

20%
51–100 Shares

18%
26–50
Shares

Source: *General Motors Public Interest Report,* 1980.

Line graphs show change over a period of time or a cause-effect relation-ship. In analyzing a line graph, you must consider the categories on both the vertical and horizontal axes and how the line, which is usually diagonal, connects the two axes. The example here shows the relationship of petroleum demand and production over a period of seventy years. Study this graph and:

1. Determine when demand will exceed production.
2. Think about ways this trend has been or could be reversed.

Tables are often used to present facts and figures in a concise manner. Using tables, an author can present a large amount of data in a small amount of space. The reader can quickly make comparisons and draw generalizations from the material.

• • • • • • • • • • • • • • • • •
World Petroleum Outlook.

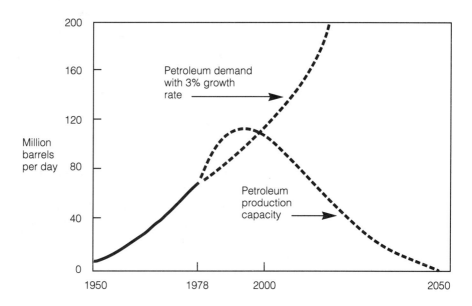

Source: *General Motors Public Interest Report,* 1980.

Maps are also useful graphics. Common in history, geography, and geology courses, they are also used in other courses. Maps can show the physical relationships of various items such as countries, regions, or states. They also show the physical characteristics of terrain as well as aerial views. Maps provide a compressed visual image of features that are impossible or very difficult to view in reality.

In general, graphics are useful for the following reasons:

1. A large amount of data can be compressed into a small amount of space.
2. The reader can quickly compare and contrast facts, figures, and other information would be boring and confusing to read in sentence form.
3. Graphics break up the monotony of the printed page.
4. They provide a visual image that is often easier to remember than words.

As reader and learner, you must make good use of any graphics available in the textbook. It is not unusual for instructors to develop test questions from these graphics.

A READING STRATEGY

The following strategy may be useful in guiding you to more effective reading. The steps in this strategy are:

1. *Before reading a chapter, survey it* by doing the following:
   a. Look over the headings to see what the chapter contains.
   b. Check to see if there are review questions at the end of the chapter. If so, read these before you read the chapter because you will have identified some of the important material ahead of time.
   c. Check to see if the chapter contains a glossary of terms. If so, read the definitions because knowing the terminology will improve your concentration while reading.
   d. Check for graphs, diagrams, charts, illustrations, or other visuals. Glance over these quickly to obtain the general intention.
   e. Read the chapter summary because this will serve as an overview.

2. *Before you start to read, formulate a few objectives* to identify what you want to learn from the chapter. These can be adapted from the questions at the end of the chapter or from an overview at the beginning of the chapter. Sometimes authors spell out objectives for the reader at the beginning of a chapter.

3. *Read a section.* If the sections are long — say, two or three pages — you may want to read only a part of a section. It is better, however, if you can read an entire section because your thinking process will be better connected.

4. *Think about what you have read.* After reading a section of the chapter, stop and reflect on what you have read. What are the major points? Are there any specific facts you can't remember? Read over your objectives and see if anything in the section is related to them. Read the questions at the end of the chapter. Were any answered in this section?

5. *Take notes.* After having read a section and reflected on what you have read and questioned yourself about the material, you are ready to take notes. Taking notes at this point in time will almost ensure that you are noting the important parts of the section.

6. *Read the remainder of the chapter.* Continue reading, reflecting and noting the remainder of the chapter.

7. *Review your notes.* After you have read the entire chapter as indicated, read over your notes. Is anything fuzzy? Do you need to reread a section? Can you answer all the questions at the end of the chapter? Do you feel comfortable with your knowledge?

Try using the strategy outlined here. If you follow it and have decent concentration, you will remember much more of the material you read.

Review

The nature of your motivation and your ability to concentrate equally affect your ability to be an effective reader. If your motivation is inappropriate and your concentration is poor, you can work to improve both.

It is important to have specific aims in mind when you read because those aims will help direct and focus your reading effort. You will probably be a more effective reader if you use various types of reading techniques such as scanning, rapid reading, and reading for depth comprehension. You must also be able to read for both literal and inferential comprehension. Finally, don't overlook graphics in your reading material because they can be valuable assets to your comprehension.

Review Questions

1. How can having both short-term and long-term goals enhance your motivation?

2. What normal distractions do you encounter when you read? Make a list of those distractions and figure out how you can overcome them.

3. What are two ways you can improve concentration while reading?

4. What are the purposes of surveying?

5. What is the difference between literal and inferential comprehension?

6. What is the difference between the analysis and synthesis levels of learning?

7. What are the three common types of graphs? For what purpose is each used?

References

Bloom, Benjamin S., Ed. *Taxonomy of Educational Objectives.* New York: David McKay, 1956.

Ostrander, Sheila and Lynn Schroeder. *Superlearning.* New York: Dell, 1979.

For Further Reading

Adler, Mortimer and Charles Van Doren. *How to Read a Book.* New York: Simon & Schuster, 1972.

Altick, Richard and Andrea Lunsford. *Preface to Critical Reading.* New York: Holt, Rinehart and Winston, 1984.

Friedman, Myles and Michael Rowls. *Teaching Reading and Thinking Skills.* New York: Longman, 1980.

Leedy, Paul. *Read with Speed and Precision.* New York: McGraw-Hill, 1963.

————. *Reading Improvement for Adults.* New York: McGraw-Hill, 1956.

Sotiriou, Peter Elias. *Integration College Study Skills.* Belmont, Calif.: Wadsworth, 1984.

Williams, Robert. *Insights into Why and How to Read.* Newark, Delaware: International Reading Association, 1976.

7

WRITING PAPERS AS A KEY TO SUCCESS

• • • • •

Regardless of your college major (already decided or yet to be chosen), the probability is high that you will do a significant amount of writing throughout your undergraduate career. In fact, because there is a current nationwide emphasis upon "writing across the curriculum," chances are that you'll do a lot more writing than your professors did when they were in school. Not only will you be writing in certain required English composition courses, you'll also be writing in courses in your major, minor, and even some elective courses.

You might recall part of the ballyhoo that accompanied the development of microcomputers for home and business use several years ago: The computer, some experts said, "would make paper obsolete." In practice, however, the very opposite has occurred. Because of microcomputers and word processors, we are cranking out more written material than before; essential writing skills have become even more significant in this computerized age.

No matter what your major happens to be or what sort of career path you follow, effective writing will be important to you — important both for personal and for professional success.

Unfortunately, however, despite the importance of writing to and for everyone, evidence indicates that most people do not possess the kind of writing skills they ought to have. For example, the academic journal *Business Education Forum* (April, 1976) published the results of a survey of personnel directors of the major corporations in the United States assessing corporate America's view of job skills, possessed or needed, of current or potential employees. Two responses dealt with skills associated with writing. To a question asking why certain job applicants were not hired, the respondents gave two reasons: (1) poorly expressed reasons for wanting the job, and (2) a poorly filled-out application form. Both these problem areas, weakness in expression and incomplete or inaccurate information, demonstrate writing deficiencies.

• • • • • • • • • •

IF YOU CAN'T WRITE IT, YOU WON'T BE UNDERSTOOD.

• • • • • • • • • •

The survey respondents also indicated that a significant area needing improvement for currently employed workers was the ability to write effectively. These corporate leaders saw weaknesses in the writing skills of both present *and* prospective employees.

More recently, the National Assessment of Educational Progress issued its *Writing Report Card* (1986). Archie Lapointe, executive director, stated flatly, "Very few of our students can write well," noting that the needs of our increasingly technological society have outpaced improved student performance in recent years. The "report card" issued a hard-hitting conclusion:

Most students, majority and minority alike, are unable to write adequately except in response to the simplest of tasks. American students can write at a minimal level, but cannot express themselves well enough to ensure that their writing will accomplish the intended purpose.

Though effective writing has become more important in our society, evidence indicates that our writing skills have not kept pace. A skill level that might have served ten or twenty years ago will not be adequate as we move toward the twenty-first century. To meet that goal, you must make a commitment to improving your writing skills: developing a style that gains attention, adheres to rules of grammar and syntax, and expresses your thoughts directly and concisely.

COMMON WRITING PROBLEMS

Many college students admit that their writing skills are not what they ought to be, but they often say that (1) they don't see a reason to be concerned about this problem, or (2) they so dislike writing they have no plans for trying to improve. Those who say they see no reason to be concerned are unaware of the importance of writing—no matter what their career hopes happen to be. Regardless of your chosen career, you will have to write—business letters, reports, memos, and the like. This is true for everyone. In fact, given the ease of information production in our microcomputerized and word-processed society, you will be asked to write more than you would have been asked to a generation ago. Because you will be doing a considerable amount of writing, your success, both in and after college, will be affected by the writing skills you possess.

Because this book is not devoted exclusively to writing per se, we do not wish to go into great detail about why students so often say they don't enjoy writing. Two oft-mentioned reasons need to be considered, however. First, many students simply do not get sufficient writing practice after their early elementary-school instruction. Multiple choice and true/false exams do not provide exercises in writing, nor do oral exercises such as book reports or interpretations of literature. Many students do little compulsory writing after the sixth grade, and this gap in their background becomes apparent when writing becomes required years later during college life.

The second reason often given for lack of writing skills is absence of sufficient training. Put simply, if you have not been taught *how* to write, it is a difficult task to master by yourself. The former Secretary of Education, William Bennett, was quite critical of this lack of training, saying that students should do more writing at the elementary and secondary levels of education. If a student arrives in college with little training in effective writing skills, he/she is in for a series of challenges, especially as higher education in the United States is working more and more writing assignments into the curriculum.

Take a moment to assess your own writing skills. If they are not good, *do not* despair. If you make the efforts required, you can improve your writing habits; you can achieve success in your writing activities. The most important thing is to have the desire and commitment to make those improvements.

• • • • • • • • • •

TO GET BETTER, YOU MUST *WANT* TO GET BETTER.

• • • • • • • • • •

One of the first steps on this path is to acquire a reference book that can help you with some writing basics. For college-level writing, there are two excellent books available that you might want to examine: *Hodges' Harbrace College Handbook* (1984) and *Rules for Writers—A Brief Handbook* (1985). Both books have a similar organization that allows you to find the information you need very quickly, and both provide plenty of examples of how things should and should not be written. Either is an invaluable resource, equally as important as a dictionary when completing a written assignment.

By using such a resource, you can avoid some of the most typical writing problems or errors, including:

• sentence fragments
• run-together sentences
• incorrect or inadequate punctuation
• nonagreement of subject and verb
• incorrect use of adjectives and adverbs
• incorrect verb tense
• misuse of pronouns and antecedents
• improper idiomatic usage

Most of those errors can be corrected by learning the proper way to express your thoughts and then practicing writing correctly. After the reference handbook has shown you how to overcome those very typical grammatical errors, you need to implement those improvements in all your written assignments. Because you probably are concerned about the grades you earn in your different courses, be assured of one thing: *If you improve your writing skills, your grades will improve as well.* College teachers appreciate good writing, primarily because they get to see so little of it, so your efforts to improve your writing skills will have a positive effect on your grades.

Within this broad area of common writing problems, teachers complain most frequently about one common failing. That failing is spelling. College professors, in general, say that their students spell atrociously—at best. And most college students admit that their spelling skills leave a great deal to be desired.

You might wonder why spelling words correctly is so important. After all, if you spell "accommodate" with only one "m," people will still understand what you meant, right? So what's the big deal? In one word: credibility. Misspellings often create the impression that the writer is poorly educated, is incompetent, does not know what he or she is writing about. Granted, those impressions may be incorrect, but do you want your credibility to suffer because of misspelled words? We hope you do not.

Spelling is a problem for many people primarily because they make no effort at all to improve their spelling skills. Many use the "eyeball method": They write the word several different ways, look at each spelling, and then try to decide which version looks best. The only problem is that sometimes all the different spellings look equally correct or incorrect! That's why a dictionary can be invaluable in checking out quickly how a word should be spelled. Because you may do a lot of in-class writing, a small paperback edition like *Webster's New World Compact School and Office Dictionary* might be a good resource book to carry along with you each day. Also, to expand your vocabulary and word choice, another portable reference well worth owning is *Roget's College Thesaurus,* an alphabetical listing of words that shows you many synonyms. Both books will prove to be helpful in all your classes.

If your spelling skills are not the greatest, please don't feel overwhelmed by this problem. First, a convenient-to-carry dictionary can help you a great deal in most writing situations both in and outside the classroom. Second, although there are many thousands of words in the English language, most of us use only a small percentage of them. Therefore, improving spelling skills really involves a relatively tiny percentage of the many thousands of words in existence.

Dr. Thomas Clark Pollock has compiled research data identifying the words most often misspelled by American students. That information is presented in modified form in Table 1. If you can master the correct spelling of these 100 words, you will have improved your spelling skills significantly — and, of course, you can use this list as a permanent resource in your future writing efforts. Because you will be doing a great deal of writing throughout your college career and after, the more you do to improve your spelling habits will pay off for you — especially in enhancing your credibility as a writer with something to say.

THE "METHOD"

One of the most significant reasons that students have problems in different writing assignments is the absence of a clear method for writing. Perhaps you have had an experience similar to this:

• • • • • • • • • • • • • • • • • • •
TABLE 1   100 Misspelled Words

1. accommodate	34. height	67. professor
2. achievement	35. interest	68. profession
3. acquire	36. its	69. prominent
4. all right	37. led	70. pursue
5. among	38. lose	71. quiet
6. apparent	39. losing	72. receive
7. argument	40. marriage	73. receiving
8. arguing	41. mere	74. recommend
9. belief	42. necessary	75. referring
10. believe	43. occasion	76. repetition
11. beneficial	44. occurred	77. rhythm
12. benefited	45. occurring	78. sense
13. category	46. occurrence	79. separate
14. coming	47. opinion	80. separation
15. comparative	48. opportunity	81. shining
16. conscious	49. paid	82. similar
17. controversy	50. particular	83. studying
18. controversial	51. performance	84. succeed
19. definitely	52. personal	85. succession
20. definition	53. personnel	86. surprise
21. define	54. possession	87. technique
22. describe	55. possible	88. than
23. description	56. practical	89. then
24. disastrous	57. precede	90. their
25. effect	58. prejudice	91. there
26. embarrass	59. prepare	92. they're
27. environment	60. prevalent	93. thorough
28. exaggerate	61. principal	94. to; too; two
29. existence	62. principle	95. transferred
30. existent	63. privilege	96. unnecessary
31. experience	64. probably	97. villain
32. explanation	65. proceed	98. woman
33. fascinate	66. procedure	99. write
		100. writing

Adapted from Newman P. Birk and Genevieve B. Birk, *Understanding and Using English,* 5th ed. (Indianapolis, Ind.: Bobbs-Merrill, 1972): 457–464.

PHIL: Did you finish your paper for English Comp?

MARDI: No, I couldn't think of anything to write about. I sat in the library for over three hours just staring at a blank sheet of paper. Nothing happened.

Many students have reported the same phenomenon experienced by Mardi: They had to write something, so they sat down at a table, pulled out a sheet of paper, and then waited for "something" to happen — and the longer a person waits for something to happen, the more frustrating and unpleasant that experience is. As frustration mounts, it becomes even more difficult to think of something to write about and that blank sheet of paper looks more and more threatening.

Instead of grabbing a piece of paper and waiting for divine intervention to spur your creative thought — all of which wastes a great deal of time with often little to show for it, you need to have a well-defined method for your writing efforts, a process that takes you from generating ideas all the way through the completion of your final written product. The following is a six-step method designed to make your writing more organized and more enjoyable:

. . .

THE METHOD

1. Idea generation
2. Idea consideration
3. Outlining
4. Completion of rough draft
5. Editing/Revision
6. Completion of final draft

Though the method may feel somewhat stilted and artificial at first, once you have mastered its elements you will find that using such a method will save you a great deal of time overall and that your writing experiences will be much more rewarding and enjoyable. Let's examine each of its component separately.

1. Idea generation.

Remember Mardi? She had to write a paper for an English class but nothing came to her. She sat in the library for three hours just staring at a blank sheet of paper. Instead of staring at blank paper, you want to actively engage in the generation of ideas to write about. Ideas do not appear miraculously, they must be found, and there are three ways to do this: (a) prior information, (b) external input, and (c) brainstorming. Each way can generate ideas that will get you started on any writing assignment, and that is the biggest hurdle to overcome — getting started.

Each time you undertake a writing assignment, ask yourself what you know about the topic area. What have you read about it? Have you seen programs dealing with the topic on television? Have you ever written about that topic, or one closely related to it, before? What do *you* think about the topic? What are some of the things that interest you about it? When you are given an assigned topic, the first resource to be consulted is yourself, to mine the bits of information you already possess to get you started.

But what about those situations when a topic is not assigned to you, when you have to select it yourself? Again, the first resource to be consulted is *you*. Granted, an open writing assignment will seem more difficult, because, it seems, your choices virtually are endless. Sometimes such infinite possibilities make choosing just one seem impossible, but that is not the case. Ask yourself these questions: What do I like to do with my time? What do I enjoy the most? What do I like to read about or watch on TV? When I hear other people talking, what topics interest me and catch my attention? By determining your own interests, you can generate some fine ideas to write about. Now your writing will be easier because you'll be assured of having a topic that interests you. When a teacher assigns you a topic, you might have to write about something you don't care about. That can be a much harder task than writing about your own topic.

· · · · · · · · · ·

YOU ARE THE BEST "FIRST" SOURCE OF INFORMATION.

· · · · · · · · · ·

Remember, regardless of whether your teacher or you selects the topic, the first place to look for ideas is inside yourself — your interests, your likes and dislikes. You are the primary source for generating ideas.

A second source of information, called *external input,* comes from other people (friends, family, and other students). Remember, these folks will tell you what they are interested in, and, of course, there's no guarantee that you'll share those interests. But asking your friends, family, and other students may provide helpful ideas, so they are a source to be considered.

Additionally, consider the audience for whom the paper is intended. Will only the teacher read it? If so, what topic(s) probably would be of interest to him/her? Will your completed paper be presented (that is, read aloud) to your class? If so, what topics are of interest to them? By considering the interests and activities of your reader(s), you can use that information to generate topics to write about, by taking reader interests into account, you will produce a final product that they will find more interesting to read or listen to.

The final source of idea generation, *brainstorming,* is a technique based upon the fact that every person possesses unrealized knowledge and information on a variety of topics. You remember a great deal of information about all sorts of things from talking with others, watching television, reading books, and the like. But you are not aware of all this information you have; it largely remains hidden within your memory banks. Brainstorming is a process designed to bring that information out.

To brainstorm effectively, you need to sit down in some private location with either pen and paper or an audio tape recorder, verbalizing as many ideas and thoughts that happen to be in your mind at that time. These different, unrelated thoughts will come quickly at first, but, as your hidden knowledge is uncovered, an eventual slowing down occurs. Though this process seems strange and a bit difficult, there is no better way to generate a wide array of ideas in a short time. Most important, you are *not* to engage in a critique of the ideas as they come to mind — don't judge them, simply record them for later use. The purpose of this exercise is only to generate ideas, to give you as much material to work with as possible as you go through the six steps of the writing method.

Regardless of how you first get your ideas for writing, the important thing to remember is that this is the first step to complete. You don't want to suffer the same fate as Mardi. Ideas don't just appear magically; you have to have a method for generating those ideas you'll be writing about.

2. Idea consideration.

After you have come up with a few ideas, your next task is one of assessment, to make decisions about which idea(s) you ought to pursue. If your assignment requires research data to support your writing, this is the time to go to a library to do the necessary preliminary research. Your assessment of topics will be aided by asking these questions:

- Would this topic meet the particular requirements of the assignment?
- Am I interested in writing about this topic?
- Can I write adequately about this topic, given the nature and limitations of the assignment?
- Can I find enough information about this topic?
- Can I explain the topic clearly enough so that my reader(s) will understand what I have written?

There are, of course, many other similar questions you could ask yourself, but your goal, at a minimum, is to determine the appropriateness of the topic and whether or not you can get the necessary information about it. Too many students decide upon a topic without knowing if their library has the information they'll need, and those people waste lots of time trying to find support data. Instead, you need to do some preliminary research before you settle upon your final topic choice.

Perhaps one of the greatest difficulties students have in writing academic papers is *narrowing the scope* of their efforts, not trying to do too much in relatively little space. In an American history course, for example, it would be absurd to attempt a term paper on "the Civil War," for the size of the task would be awesome. Instead, you want to have a narrow topic that you can cover in some meaningful detail. You could do a good job describing a single battle, or discussing the conditions of the Confederate prison camp at Andersonville, or examining the political problems faced by the Democrats in the presidential election of 1864. Any of these topics could be covered in one paper; the theme of the entire Civil War cannot.

Your assessment of ideas is critical to the writing process because the viability of your topic choice directly affects the success or failure of your final written product. Just as it is impossible for a football coach to put together a winning team with poor players, so, too, is it impossible for you to produce an outstanding written product with a weak or inappropriate topic.

3. Outlining.

Once you have secured the necessary information to write about your chosen topic, you must be concerned with how to organize that information. Regardless of the organizational format you select (a topic discussed later within this chapter), it is essential that you present the information in a well-organized manner. Disorganized, sloppily presented material is difficult to read and understand — if it gets read at all. One way to help organize your thoughts is the process of outlining.

Outlining not only improves the organizational qualities of everything you write, it also helps you save time in writing the final paper by giving you a skeleton structure to follow. Here is how to do it. After you have collected all necessary research data:

- List the main ideas to be covered in your paper, then rearrange them in a logical sequence.
- Make certain that all main ideas are expressed clearly and that they are aimed at the intended reader(s).
- Arrange all subordinate ideas under the appropriate main ideas so that there is a logical flow of thought within each main idea and its subordinate development.
- Note where all research data are to be included within the structure of both main and subordinate ideas.
- Finally, recheck your entire outline to make certain that it is arranged to meet the purpose of the writing assignment and to meet the interests of the intended reader(s).

Many college students avoid outlining because it brings back unhappy memories from high school English classes where outlining often became a boring chore. Actually, outlining can be highly rewarding if you recognize its value in the overall writing process. It doesn't really matter whether you use a sentence outline or a phrase outline; the important thing is to have your ideas well organized *before* you start writing your paper. Outlining will guarantee that organization and add the bonus benefit of saving time once you actually start writing.

To check the organization of your material once you have completed your outline is, try this technique: On a sheet of paper, write or type your outline with your major and subordinate ideas clearly stated. Take scissors and cut that outline into its component parts, one idea per slip. Now give these slips of paper to a friend, asking him or her to arrange the ideas in the way they best make sense. If your friend is able to recreate your outline with the paper slips, then you know your outline is organized logically and properly. If, however, your friend's arrangement differs radically from your outline, you'd better rethink the organization you had planned to follow.

4. Completion of the rough draft.

Now that you are satisfied with the outline of your materials, you may prepare the rough draft of your paper, making it as complete a document as possible. Write your paper the way you want to present the information, following the structure of your outline and including all the research data that is pertinent. Some students prefer to compose their rough drafts with pencil and paper; others compose at the typewriter. It really doesn't matter which way you do it, as long as you are comfortable with the method you select.

You'll notice that you're at the fourth point of our six-point writing method, meaning that there is more to come. Unfortunately, however, many students stop here, after completing their rough draft. This rough draft becomes their final draft that they give the teacher. But this is a great mistake; stopping in the writing process at this point is premature. You need to refine this draft to make your final written product as smooth and error free as possible. Because you are still composing your paper at this stage, it is natural that you'll make mistakes because you're so involved in the paper-creation process. To eliminate those mistakes, you need to stay with the six-step method, recognizing that your rough draft is just that — a rough draft.

5. Editing/Revision.

This is the stage where you refine your first writing effort, where you take the "rough" out of your rough draft. You may find this step in our writing method the most difficult because it is hard to critique your own work. It is, however, something that must be done.

When you were composing your rough draft, your attention was focused on putting thoughts down on paper, the actual creation of your written product, not on fine points of grammar or spelling. Because of that, it is easy to make mistakes, to overlook obvious errors. Taking the time to edit or revise your material gives you an opportunity to correct these mistakes. Professional writers always take a second look at their material to make necessary changes, and you should do the same.

If you have great difficulty critiquing your own material, you might ask a friend to help you out, seek an outside opinion on what you have written. Newspapers, book publishing houses, and magazine publishers employ copy editors to do this sort of thing, to check for errors and make modifications in materials prepared by reporters, authors, and writers. You might find that an outside opinion will be helpful in improving the flow of your rough draft.

Regardless of whether you and/or another undertake the task of editing and revising your rough draft, remember to look for those common writing errors presented earlier within this chapter. You may use them as a checksheet when working through your rough draft.

6. Completion of the final draft.

Now you can put together your final draft, the paper you will give to your teacher. Use your edited and revised rough draft as the road map in writing your final draft, always making sure that your copy has a flow and smoothness to it.

Even if your assignment does not require you to do so, type your final paper if at all possible. A typewritten paper is neater, cleaner, and generally more impressive than a handwritten one. Because much of how a reader reacts to written material is impressionistic, you want to create as favorable an impression as possible—especially if a grade is riding on the outcome. A neatly typed paper, free of typing errors and smudges, will help to create the impression you want. Just as we react more positively toward a man wearing a coat and tie rather than a sweatshirt and jeans, so, too, do we react better to a typewritten paper.

If you follow the six-step writing method, from idea generation to completion of your final draft, you will find that your papers are better organized, have a better word and thought flow, and that you will save time in the writing process in the long run. Once you have completed your necessary research, you should be able to produce a final version of your paper within seven to ten days. The method may appear cumbersome at first, but after using it a few times, you will find it has become a very natural way of writing for you—both inside and outside the classroom.

WRITING FOR DIFFERENT PURPOSES

Given current pressures on and priorities within our colleges and universities, there is no doubt that you will be asked to write a number of papers throughout your college career. Because this emphasis on encouraging more student writing will not subside for quite some time (if ever), you can count on doing large amounts of writing in many of your classes. Writing, however, is not just writing; a writing assignment in one class will not necessarily be the same as one in another class. You must be flexible in your writing to meet the demands of different writing *purposes,* for the specific purpose of each writing assignment will determine how you should go about completing it.

Overall, there are three different purposes for communicating with others, whether we are engaged in oral or written communication:

1. To inform someone about something ("How the internal combustion engine works").

2. To persuade someone about something ("The United States should continue to aid the Nicaraguan rebels").

3. To entertain someone ("How to lose $100 in ten minutes in Las Vegas").

All communication efforts are aimed at one, or a combination, of those three purposes. Most of your written work, however, will emphasize the first two purposes (although you would hope that all your writing would be somewhat entertaining and enjoyable for the reader!).

Here is a list of the different kinds of writing assignments you may expect at the undergraduate level:

Term Papers. The most commonly assigned written exercises, regardless of major or course of study, term papers are generally research oriented, meaning that you will have to spend some time in a library gathering the specific information you need to document your conclusions. Such papers may be purely *informative* in nature, explaining some facet of a topic pertinent to your class, or they may be *persuasive,* requiring you to argue a point of view throughout the paper. Term papers can be rather lengthy, requiring a major course-long effort on your part to put together a viable result: Hence the name, which suggests the amount and length of effort required: "term paper."

Critical Analyses. The word *critical* indicates that you must make some sort of judgment on what you have written about, a topic that can range across the entire curricular spectrum. You may be asked to make a critical analysis of a Presidential speech, a play, a painting, a proposed visitation policy for campus dormitories, a book or magazine article, a theory — almost anything. The important factor to remember here is that you are expected to render a decision, some sort of value judgment that indicates something is good, bad, just, unjust, moral, immoral, and so on. Therefore, your purpose as a writer is to make certain that your thesis is clear and that your paper is structured to support your thesis statement.

Reports. A written report is primarily an informational statement about something, including laboratory or field experiments you might have conducted as part of a class. A report should be designed to let the reader know *what* happened and *why,* providing sufficient information to make him or her feel a part of the process that took place. You probably had to do book reports in high school — an informational analysis covering what the book was about, whether or not it achieved its purpose, whether it was interesting to read. Such student reports seem to be growing in popularity in higher education, too, often accompanied by an oral presentation to the rest of the class. So you can expect to write several different types of reports while in college.

One type is called "media reviews," an analysis of a film, a play, a television program, a radio show. Media reviews are a combination of the two previously mentioned categories, critical analyses and reports; they often require that you describe the event (report), then criticize its value (critical analysis), primarily from your own perspective. Though you may use research information to support your own conclusions (e.g., citing the review of the same film by the media critic of the *New York Times*), a media review primarily represents a personal judgment.

Creative Writing. In various humanities and fine arts classes you may be assigned creative writing projects — poetry, short stories, prose essays, and the like. Although there may be certain rules to follow (length of a story; structure or rhythm of a poem), you are given great latitude in completing the assignment because it is entirely personal in nature. You do not need research information to support points; you need no outside information at all. Creative writing is a personal written expression of something you feel inside — it is purely "creative." Though you have great freedom, however, you are still expected to follow the guidelines of effective writing expected in every assignment.

When you are given a writing assignment, then, you must first determine the purpose of that assignment, for the purpose will let you know how to proceed. Because not all assignments are the same, it is important that you be purpose oriented as you undertake each assignment. By the time you complete your college career, you'll find that you have written a lot of different papers fulfilling a multiplicity of purposes.

PREPARING AND PRODUCING A PAPER

Following the "method" used throughout this process, once you have determined the purpose of your writing assignment, have picked the topic, and then have completed all necessary information gathering (research), you finally come to the point of writing your paper. In preparing your paper, you *must* focus on organization, especially in actually structuring your thoughts and sequencing them in some sort of logical order. Remember that organization is vitally important to the reader(s). Not only is disorganized thought difficult to understand, but your reader(s) may not even try to read material that lacks organization — and thus your grade may suffer.

Overall, your paper will follow this structure:

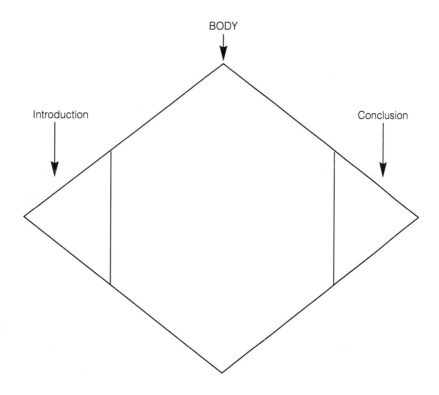

If nothing else, visualizing each writing assignment in this way reemphasizes the notion of cohesive structure. Everything within the paper must interrelate, everything within the paper must build on all the other elements, or the structure itself will fall apart. Let's briefly examine each of the major units of our writing structure.

The Introduction

The *Introduction* is designed to accomplish two goals: (1) to catch the reader's attention, and (2) to indicate to the reader the purpose of the paper. After reading the introduction, the reader should have a very clear idea about what your paper is about and what he or she should expect from reading it. The introduction previews your paper, and an effective introduction previews the main points to be developed. The exact length of an introduction varies a bit from paper to paper depending upon its length and content, but in general about 5 percent of your paper should be introductory material. A ten-page paper (one of the commonest lengths in college assignments) calls for an introduction of less than one page.

The Body

After getting your reader interested and previewing your paper's main points in the introduction, you move on to the *body* of your manuscript. This is where you will achieve your purpose of informing, and/or, persuading, and/or entertaining your reader(s) about your topic. This is where you present the bulk of your analysis and research data, and consequently this is where most of your time and effort will be spent. In general, 85 percent of your paper's total length should be the body of the paper, or between eight and nine pages of a ten-page paper.

Because it will have to sustain reader interest and idea clarity for so many pages, it is vitally important that the body of your paper be organized very carefully. The internal structure of the body should be determined by the content of the paper and what your overall purpose is. These are the main internal structures from which you have to choose:

1. *Deductive or Anticlimax.* In this organizational pattern, the most important material/information is presented first, with the remainder of the paper devoted to supporting that initial point. This structure is favored in journalism classes because it corresponds to the way that stories appear in newspapers. The idea is that readers have little time to spend reading a newspaper, so the lead paragraph in the story gives the basic information that the reader needs to know; the rest of the material provides additional detailed information that can be read at a later time. The deductive or anticlimax structure is most applicable for shorter papers you may write; it is a difficult kind of organization to use in longer writing assignments.

2. *Inductive or Climax.* Some people refer to this organizational pattern as "logical" because it follows the logical sequence of going from one point to another, building to one overall conclusion. The inductive structure is a building-block process in which each point builds upon the preceding point, culminating in the major point you want your reader(s) to remember. You are probably most familiar with this type of organization, since much of human reasoning follows the "A-to-B-to-C-to-conclusion" approach. You will find that the inductive structure is well suited for long written assignments as well as for papers designed to be primarily persuasive in nature.

3. *Chronological.* This time-related organization allows you to write about how something has happened or developed over time. If your topic has time as a critical factor, the chronological structure might be the most appropriate organization to follow. In writing an informative report on a laboratory experiment in your chemistry class, for example, you could proceed by highlighting the most important developments in your experiment as they occurred, day by day or even hour by hour.

4. *Comparison-Contrast.* This pattern, more specialized than the preceding ones, requires you to write about two objects (or more), delineating how they are alike (comparison) and/or how they are different (contrast). You may compare and contrast virtually anything, recognizing that the more the objects are alike, the easier it is to draw comparisons, and the more the objects are not alike, the easier it is to write about contrasts.

5. *Extended Example or Process Progression.* This could be called the "how-to" structure because it allows you to describe how to do something or how something works. For example, you might write a paper concerning how to go about opening a savings account at a bank. Your organization would follow a step-by-step process of the things a person would do to get the job done. You see many examples of this structure in training manuals and materials instructions, the purpose of which is to give your reader sufficient information to perform a certain task. (We should add that writing clear instructional information is a great skill — as anyone who has tried to assemble a child's swingset from printed instructions can attest!)

6. *Spatial.* This final organizational pattern is the most specialized and one you will have the least tendency to use. *Spatial structure* refers to the relationship of objects in space. This pattern allows you to develop a visual image of a physical object through the use of words, perhaps supplemented by pictures or drawings. If you were to describe the physical layout of a house, for example, you might describe the size and shape of the living room, explaining its physical relationship to the location of the kitchen, to the family room, and so on.

Again, as you prepare to write your paper, you must let its content and purpose determine which of the preceding internal organizations you select. Although you will find that one of those patterns is the most comfortable for you, not all papers can be written following that same pattern. You need to be flexible enough to use the pattern most appropriate for each writing assignment.

Since 85 percent of your paper will be devoted to body development, you must be concerned with the most basic elements that make up that development. If you look upon all writing as a building-block process, then you will see how all elements within the process can fit together, principally the elements of words, sentences, and paragraphs. For detailed information regarding those elements of style, you are encouraged to refer to an English composition text, but here are a few bits of information to help you in the most basic areas.

The smallest unit of thought in our language system is the individual *word*. Some words are relatively unimportant in terms of meaning ("the"), but they allow us to express ourselves grammatically. Other words are ripe with all possible meanings (''bastard''); these words give our language color and richness. Words do not mean the same thing to all people, however, so you must choose your words very carefully. Even the simplest of words can conjure up widely divergent meanings or impressions. If you don't believe that, ask ten of your friends to define the word ''gay''; you might be surprised by the different definitions to such a simple three-letter word. Because the word is our first building block, it must be selected with care and precision. Sloppy word choice is to be avoided.

The next element of composition is the collection of words into a complete *sentence,* for the structure of the sentence allows you to offer a cohesive thought to your reader. Just as you must be careful in choosing words to express your thoughts, so too must you exercise care in putting your sentences together. Specifically, there are three major types of sentence patterns — direct, indirect, and balanced — each of which you may use depending on the nature of thought to be expressed.

The simplest sentence pattern, called *direct,* is structured simply: noun-verb-object. For example, ''The experiment has failed,'' is a direct sentence. You'll note that the point made is a simple one, and that its presentation is direct and straightforward.

The *indirect* sentence, often disliked by language purists, gives you the opportunity to explain something before offering the conclusionary point near the end of the sentence: ''Because the results of the study did not meet our expectations, we conclude that the experiment has failed.'' The indirect structure is a good one when you find it necessary to offer explanatory or qualifying information before making a certain point. Some teachers, however, have a bias against this type of sentence structure, so it is one that ought to be used with care.

The *balanced* sentence, sometimes referred to as the compound sentence, allows you to combine two different but related thoughts into one sentence instead of writing two separate sentences: ''We thought the experiment might be successful, yet we found our expectations were not met.''

No one sentence pattern is better than another. Each is stylistically acceptable and useful for a writer. Having that choice, however, allows you to make composition decisions that will make your paper more interesting to your reader(s). By varying the types of sentences used throughout your paper, you will be able to maintain reader interest, for a ten-page paper consisting of one direct sentence after another becomes boring. If you use all three sentence types, the variety in sentence structure alone will make your paper more interesting and readable, so use a variety of sentences if at all possible.

Similarly, you also want to vary the length of sentences throughout your paper. You are probably aware that we tend to write in longer sentences than we speak. In writing, the reader can go back to something unclear in a long sentence, but there is no rereading option in oral communication. So you'll find that your writing style differs from your oral style just in the nature in the length of sentences used to communicate your thoughts. Don't make the mistake of writing like you speak. Sentences of the same length, whether long or short, become visually boring to the reader(s). Just as with sentence selection, to maintain reader interest, you need to vary sentence length. This is especially important when your paper is ten pages or more in length.

The final element of composition is the *paragraph,* the collection of sentences centering on one particular point. There are no rules for (1) length of a paragraph, or (2) the number of paragraphs each of your papers ought to have. Such rules would be a silly waste of time. Instead, remember that a paragraph is supposed to be confined to one major thought development. When you change thoughts or ideas, it is time to create a new paragraph to maintain thought clarity for your reader(s).

We encourage you to use an English composition reference book like those mentioned earlier. Such a reference book will help you make decisions about style and structure, the goal being to make your thoughts clear and compelling and your final written product interesting and readable. By exercising care in making decisions about word choice and sentence and paragraph structuring, you'll find that your papers are better — both from a compositional standpoint as well as from the interested reader's standpoint.

One final element needs to be considered in developing the body of your paper: the use of visuals. Charts, graphs, maps, sketches, pictures, and other visuals can be used effectively to improve the clarity of your written presentation. Because many people are visual learners, these visual aids inherently attract their attention and interest. Do not, however, overdo a good thing. Instead follow these suggestions in deciding to use visuals in your papers:

1. Visuals should support what you have written, not attempt to take the place of your analysis. Your paper must be more than merely a collection of visuals tied together by a title page.

2. All visuals must be an integral part of your paper, not something thrown in to take up space.

3. Visuals should be simple and clear in structure. A confusing visual only makes the situation worse.

4. Each visual should contain enough information to be fairly self-explanatory. Remember, the visual is there to help explain what you have written; your paper is not supposed to be an explanation of your visuals.

5. If possible, consider the use of color in presenting your visuals. Color can add both visual variety and greater informational clarity for your reader.

The Conclusion

The final unit of construction in our writing structure is the conclusion, where you must tie everything together. Many inexperienced writers do not spend enough time in developing their conclusions; they often come to the end of a sentence and stop, leaving the reader dangling in mid-air. You don't want to do that.

The best way to think of putting a conclusion together is to summarize the main points developed within your paper, those ideas you want the reader to remember. Because the conclusion is the last thing your reader will read, this is your final chance to reemphasize those points that were of greatest importance throughout. In general, about 10 percent of your paper's total length should be devoted to the conclusion, or about one page of the typical ten-page paper. You thus have the time and space necessary to write a solid summary statement that highlights your most important material.

Review

Because of the increasing emphasis on writing in colleges and universities, you are guaranteed to do a great deal of writing throughout your college career, regardless of academic major or desired career choice. To be as effective a writer as possible, you need to adopt a clear method for putting your papers together. This chapter suggested a six-step writing method: (1) idea generation, (2) idea consideration, (3) outlining, (4) completion of rough draft, (5) editing/revision, and (6) completion of final draft. This method will save you time and produce organized papers with improved word and thought flow.

Though you may be asked to write different types of papers (term papers, critical analyses, reports, and creative writing), all your papers must be well organized in their presentation of material. The writing structure of introduction, body, and conclusion forms a cohesive organizational pattern that makes your writing clear and readable. In constructing your paper, you must be concerned with its internal organizational elements as well as with word choice, structure and length of sentences and paragraphs, and possible use of visuals to explain difficult content. You are encouraged to use an English composition reference book to help you complete the final drafts of your papers.

Review Questions

1. What type of writing do you *like* to read? Who are some of your favorite writers? Can you get some ideas from those writings and writers that might make you a better writer?

2. What has been your greatest difficulty in writing papers to date? What steps are you planning to undertake to overcome or reduce that difficulty?

3. How would you assess your writing skills after trying to use the "method" described in this chapter? Did you find that your approach to a writing assignment became more organized and methodical?

References

Business Education Forum, "Results of National Employees' Survey." April, 1976.

Hacker, Diana. *Rules for Writers — A Brief Handbook.* New York: St. Martin's Press, 1985.

Hodges, John C. and Mary E. Whitten. *Hodges' Harbrace College Handbook,* 9th ed. New York: Harcourt Brace Jovanovich, 1984.

National Assessment of Educational Progress. *The Writing Report Card.* Princeton, N.J.: Educational Testing Service, 1986.

For Further Reading

Kennedy, X. J. and Dorothy M. Kennedy. *The Bedford Reader.* 2nd ed. New York: St. Martin's Press, 1985.

Mansfield, J. and S. Bahniuk. *Writing Business Letters and Reports.* Indianapolis, Ind.: Bobbs-Merrill Educational Publishing, 1981.

Wyld, Lionel D. *Preparing Effective Reports.* New York: Odyssey Press, 1967.

C H A P T E R 8

EXAMS AS A
KEY TO SUCCESS

Threpurpose of this chapter is to provide you with added understanding of:

1. The importance of exams in college
2. Tips for preparing for exams
3. Types of exams commonly used
4. Tips on taking various types of exams

Imperfect as they may be, instructor-made exams are the basis for final grades in many college courses. Part of the education you receive in college is learning how to translate and transfer what you know into the knowledge format required by your instructors. It is not unusual for a student to fail an exam for reasons other than lack of knowledge. Some common causes for doing poorly on exams include misinterpreting questions, inadvertently omitting part of a question, or organizing material poorly. Therefore, besides knowing the content, knowing how to take exams is helpful to your overall success in college.

THE IMPORTANCE OF EXAMS

Success in college is measured by the academic record you build, which is derived from the grades you receive in various courses. That academic record is yours—you earn the grades that made it and you can't get rid of it even if you try. It will follow you around like an angel or the plague depending on how good or bad it is. If you apply for graduate school, you will have to produce a transcript of your grades; a copy of your transcript also goes in the college placement file that potential employers can see. It makes sense, then, to develop as good an academic record as you possibly can.

Although instructors vary in the way they weigh exams in relation to the course grade, it is probably rare for exams to count less than 50 percent of the course grade, but it is not unusual for exams to count as much as 75 percent or 100 percent of the course grade. In most cases, however, the course grade usually consists of some combination of exams, short quizzes, written papers, laboratory work, oral reports, and class participation. In cases where multiple bases are used for determining a grade, you need to find out the relative weight of each base in relation to the course grade. This knowledge will help you establish priorities and put your time and emphasis on the factors that have the greatest impact on your grade; otherwise you could spend a great deal of time on an assignment that counts in the end for very little.

Information about the relative importance of assignments and grades should be contained in the course syllabus, but if it isn't, ask the instructor. If you happen to be a poor test taker and the instructor weights exams heavily, you may have to work hard at improving your ability to perform on exams. It is possible to compensate somewhat for poor performance on exams by doing exceptionally well on other assignments, if those are meaningful in the grade calculation. It is very unlikely, however, that you can perform poorly on all the exams and still receive an acceptable grade even with an outstanding performance on other assignments. Thus, doing well on exams is important to the academic record you build and to your overall success in college.

Students sometimes argue that a grade is not an accurate reflection of the quantity or quality of their learning in a given course. This is probably true and professors are likely to agree with the argument. Further, many professors would admit that their exams are not perfectly constructed and don't necessarily measure what you know. But what do these admissions accomplish for you? It may make you feel better to convince yourself that a grade does not indicate what you learned in a course, but that isn't going to change a low grade. An exam grade is an indicator of how well you demonstrate *the knowledge the instructor chooses to include in an exam.* Accurate or inaccurate, that grade will stand as the indicator of your knowledge.

The importance of exams, or at least of a single exam, can vary with the type of term division your college uses. The *quarter* system usually consists of ten-week terms; the semester system has fifteen weeks. As you can see, two semesters equal three quarters in terms of total weeks spent in classes. Because individual quarters are much shorter, however, the number of exams in this type of term will be fewer. The fewer the number of exams, the more it will hurt if you flunk one. Suppose you are attending college under the quarter system and you have an instructor who gives only a mid-term and a final as the basis for the grade. Further, suppose you flunk the mid-term. What are your chances of receiving a decent grade in the course? Even if you pull an A on the final, your chances of a grade better than a C are slim unless the final is weighed much heavier. Many professors understand this dilemma and try to give two exams and other assignments in addition to the final.

Because a semester is five weeks longer than a quarter, you are likely to have more exams under that system. Most instructors under the semester system give a mid-term, a final and two other exams; some, however, may give as many as five. Other instructors may give only three, with each falling at the end of a five-week period. Again, it is important to know the weight assigned to each exam. Where four exams are given, the final may count 40 percent, the mid-term 30 percent, and each of the other exams 15 percent each of the final grade. In that arrangement, two exams would be considered major and two minor. Flunking one of the minor exams might not be disastrous, but by the same token an A on a minor exam would not compensate for a poor grade on a major exam.

STUDYING FOR EXAMS

"I don't know how to study for that chemistry exam," or "I don't know what to study for that economics exam," are fairly common statements made by college students. These are normal dilemmas, but dilemmas that can be reduced by applying a few simple tips while preparing for exams. Tips about preparing for exams are given throughout this book, but they will be consolidated in this section. Keep in mind that these suggestions are only that and may not constitute the perfect strategy for you to use in preparing for exams. You should develop your own strategy for studying—a strategy that fits the way *you* think and function. Yet you must also recognize that for exams in some courses you may have to depart from your favorite method. Many students have probably flunked out of college because they failed to change an unsuccessful method of studying for exams.

Successful methods of exam study vary from person to person. They may also vary in terms of the nature of the subject. In some subject areas it is necessary to know the facts; in others, you may need to know the facts in a certain order; in still others, you may need to relate or apply the facts. Yet any of these statements could apply to any subject area. Another variable in your preparation is the known or perceived concerns of the instructor. What does the instructor want you to know—facts, main ideas, or both? Further, consider your own strengths as you prepare for exams. Can you remember facts easily? Are principles easy for you to remember? Can you tie thoughts together to form an essay? Recognizing your strengths and weaknesses can help you to study more effectively. Perhaps the following study tips will help you.

1. Begin preparing for exams when you attend the first lecture or read the first chapter of the text.

As you listen to lectures and read the text, say to yourself: "If I were teaching this course, would I use that fact or idea for an exam question?" If you think so, put an asterisk by your note or at the appropriate place in the text. Of course, you will not be able to predict with 100 percent or even 50 percent accuracy, but you will not be hurt unless you limit your study to only those items you have predicted will be test questions. The important thing is to *think exam,* but don't let those thoughts consume your attention. The simple process of thinking exam as you listen and read will help that material become better entrenched in your brain.

2. Study carefully the emphasized material.

We stress this in the chapter on notetaking, but it is important enough to mention again. If you have marked emphasized material in your notes and the text, make sure you know that material before taking an exam. Get that material firmly entrenched in your mind because it is important. Other material will probably be related to it, too, because one bit of material serves as a stimulus to remember another bit. Once you get this *chaining* process going, assuming that the material is systematically tied together, you can pass any test. Chaining is probably a most useful technique in subjects such as math, physics, chemistry, and other courses where *A* is related to *B* is related to *C*, and so on.

3. Know the type of test you will be taking.

Instructors will generally tell you if an exam is going to be objective, subjective, or some combination of the two. If an instructor does not tell you, *ask*. In general, you will probably need to study differently for an objective exam than you will for a subjective exam. In fact, it is important to know the type of exams early in the term because such knowledge could change the way you listen and read. If exams are going to be objective, you know that facts, dates, names, places, events, formulae, and specialized terms may be very important. If, however, the exam is to be essay, you will have to know the same material as for the objective exam plus various possibilities related to application.

4. Study your notes and hi-lited text items carefully.

If you have done a reasonably good job of taking notes and hi-liting in the text, you should have identified all the basic material you need to study for an exam. You may not know if you have hi-lited and noted properly until after the first exam, in which case you may need to make some quick adjustments. Read your notes on a regular basis, not just the night before an exam. A good plan is to read your notes each day after you have recorded them. Then about twice each week read all the cumulative notes. About four or five days before an exam, start reading your notes daily. Use the same plan for hi-lited material in the text. If you follow this schedule, you will not have to cram the night before an exam and will probably perform much better. As you read, look away from your notes or text and talk aloud, reciting both major points and details; you can also close your eyes and silently review the material. You can develop a set of flash cards with questions on one side and answers on the other and run through those a number of times before an exam. Whatever method you use, mentally *intend* to remember the material you are studying. Don't review the material in a mechanical, impersonal way and expect to remember it well.

5. Memorize some material.

Memorization was once a common learning device in elementary and high school, but it was deemphasized with the advent of progressive teaching methods. As is often the case with change, the useful aspects of memorization were thrown out with the nonuseful. The truth is that memorization is very useful for certain kinds of material and you should memorize if you are able to use that technique effectively. You may need to know a formula or a list of items to be able to respond to questions that require you to use a factual base. It would be a shame to know how to apply a formula but be unable to demonstrate that knowledge because you had forgotten the formula itself. Material you will use time after time is what you may want to commit to memory. If, for example, you plan to major in chemistry, memorizing the table of elements and the symbols would probably be of great benefit.

6. Use mnemonic devices.

Using mnemonic devices is somewhat like memorizing, but with this technique you associate the material you want to remember with something common in your life or with a catchy phrase. For example, if you needed to know when Roosevelt was first elected President (1932) and your father was also born in that year, association of the two events might help you remember the date. If you need to remember a list of items, try to make a word out of the first letter of each item in the list. The possibilities for creating mnemonic devices are endless, if this technique appeals to you (see Chapter 3).

7. Relate facts to principles as you study.

To be prepared for any kind of test, learn facts and principles together if both are presented in the subject you are studying. Read the facts and then the principle, then reverse the process. Do this a number of times until those associations are strong. You are then prepared for either an objective or an essay exam.

8. Study with someone.

Some students find it helpful to study with other students from the same course. This method allows you to ask each other questions, give explanations of material you understand, and receive explanations of material you don't understand. Sometimes you can understand material better when a peer presents it than when an instructor does. If you study with one or two other persons, try to select study partners who appear to know at least as much about the subject as you do; or, if possible, select partners who know more than you do. It is also a good idea to select a partner who thinks differently—that is, takes a different approach to learning the material—because this new perspective may help you learn more effectively. Don't let your study group get too large, though; there is more likelihood of its turning into a social club if too many are involved.

9. Develop self-confidence.

Self-confidence is as important to success in taking exams as in all other life endeavors. Study properly and study enough and you can enter the exam with the gut feeling that you know the material and can perform well. Self-confidence is important and can provide you an advantage, but by itself it is not enough. Some solid studying will help you develop an appropriate level of self-confidence. *Don't delude yourself*—don't tell yourself you know the material when deep down you know you don't. Be realistic about your level of knowledge and your ability to deliver that knowledge. If you tell yourself that you know the material but continually make grades of C and D on exams, you are practicing self-delusion and relying on false self-confidence.

TYPES OF EXAMS

Basically, two types of exams are used to demonstrate knowledge in university courses. One type is called *objective* and consists of questions in the true/false, multiple choice, and matching varieties. The second is called *subjective* and consists of essay and short answer questions. This classification of exams is actually based on the method of evaluation rather than the method of construction. Objective exams have clear-cut, correct answers and instructors grade them objectively; because there is only one right answer, they have no decisions to make during the grading process. On the other hand, the essay exam is subjective because instructors make decisions about the quality of the response during the grading process. There is, of course, subjectivity involved in the so-called objective exam. That subjectivity is in the selection process an instructor uses to choose items for the exam; there are few guidelines and no rules for what should be covered on an exam, and that remains almost totally the choice of an instructor. In reality, then, the so-called objective exam is objective only in the way it is scored. With this qualification, we can now turn to a closer examination of these two types of exams.

OBJECTIVELY EVALUATED EXAMS

Exams evaluated objectively can contain questions of a number of types, but the most common seem to be multiple choice, true/false, matching, word completion, and questions that can be answered with one or two sentences. Of these types, multiple choice is probably the most often used and we will examine it first.

Multiple Choice Questions

Some students call multiple choice questions "multiple guess," but if they are properly developed, multiple choice questions can be extremely difficult.

Good multiple choice questions can tap higher levels of learning just as essay questions do. You should not underestimate how tough multiple choice questions can be and thereby fail to study enough. Because of the ease of computer scoring, multiple choice exams are probably more popular now than ever, so it is important that you learn how to take them well.

Multiple choice questions consist of a *stem*, which is the lead part of the statement, and usually four to six *response choices* to complete the stem. One of those responses can be a *seductive alternative*—that is, a response designed for the purpose of misleading the student who does not know the material. The seductive alternative seems to be the logical choice—especially to those whose knowledge is shallow. Some instructors also include a response that is so far out in left field it isn't even related to the topic. The correct answer is obviously one of the remaining responses. If you know the answer to a question, you won't be taken in by the purposeful attempts to mislead you. If you don't know the answer, however, use a process of elimination. Find the seductive alternative first, then see if there is a response that does not seem to be related to the topic. You will win a few and lose a few with a process of elimination, but it beats mere guessing.

Some instructors use *response alternatives: none of the above, all of the above, a and b above, c and d above, a and c above* or *b and d above.* Some students find these response categories very confusing. The response *all of the above* clearly means that the response choices have to be somewhat alike. Likewise, the response alternatives *a and b* or *a and c* should have some common elements, so look for the one that doesn't fit. If *b* seems to be odd man out, select *a* and *c*. In the case of *none of the above,* if the responses seem to be alike chances are good that this is the correct response.

In general, look for clues given inadvertently in the stem. Is there a key word that suggests the correct response? Besides the question stem itself, you should learn to look for clues in other questions on the same exam. An unfamiliar technical term included in the responses for one question might be present—perhaps even defined—in the stem of another question. If the exam contains other types of items such as true/false or matching, look for clues in those sections.

True-False Questions

For some students, true/false questions provide an opportunity to beat the professor at his own game. A high school student who probably never made over a D in his high school career chose true for every question on a 100-item true/false test in civics. You guessed it. There were only two false questions on the entire test and George received his only A in high school. Some experts believe true/false tests do not measure much in terms of knowledge because astute students can answer some questions without knowing the content. What are some characteristics of true/false questions?

1. Teachers tend to construct more true statements overall on these exams than false statements. If you simply can't determine the correct response, mark the statement true.

2. Statements containing words such as *usually, often, seldom,* or *rarely* seem to be true more often than false.

3. True statements are usually longer than false statements because the true statement may need a qualifier.

4. Questions containing words such as *all, none, always,* or *never* are usually false because there is very little in this world that can be described in such absolute terms.

Whether you are dealing with true/false or multiple-choice questions, always be sure to read the entire statement or question before responding. Sometimes students read the stem in a multiple choice question, then read and select the first response, A, without reading the other responses. Read all responses carefully, especially if the instructor directs you to select the best response. Likewise with true/false statements, read the entire statement before responding. Don't be misled by the first part of a statement, which may seem to be solidly true. One general rule for any kind of objective question is to complete the ones you are certain of so that you will have time enough to get through the exam. After completing those, go back to the ones you didn't know or weren't sure about and try to figure out the correct answers. Another general rule is to read all directions carefully because an instructor may have slightly different directions than those you have followed on previous tests.

Matching Questions

Here are a few suggestions to keep in mind when responding to a matching exercise on an exam:

1. There may be a different number of items in the two columns of items to be matched, so don't expect the two columns to come out even.

2. Some items in one column can be used more than once.

3. Matching exercises usually contain seductive alternatives to mislead you purposely.

If you are uncertain, do the ones you know and then use a process of elimination. Matching exercises sometimes have strange directions, so make sure you read the directions and understand the process.

SUBJECTIVELY EVALUATED EXAMS

You may have a mental set for or against essay exams as a result of experiences in high school. Some students prefer the type of mental process necessary for writing essay exams; others prefer the mental process involved in taking objective exams. If you perform well on an essay exam, fine. If you don't, it would be to your advantage to learn how to take them.

Some students mistakenly label ''essay'' any question for which they have to produce the information. It is true that you must produce information to respond to an essay question, but you must also produce information for some objectively evaluated questions. If, for example, you are asked to list five causes of the Civil War, you are clearly producing the data, but that question would be evaluated objectively. There is a correct response—you either can or cannot list five causes of the Civil War. Instructor judgment would enter into the evaluation of this response little if at all.

Why do instructors use essay questions? For a number of reasons, such as determining:

1. If students can demonstrate understanding of the material.
2. If students can apply the material to other situations.
3. If students can analyze ideas or principles.
4. If students can put facts or ideas together or show how facts may contribute to a principle or concept.
5. If students can evaluate information, ideas, or principles.
6. If students can write a coherent paper.

Instructors who use essay questions for any of these reasons are trying to ascertain your ability to think at higher levels. They are not satisfied with your knowledge of the facts alone; they want a demonstration of your ability to apply knowledge. Because essay questions are more complicated than objectively evaluated questions, some tips for responding are suggested below.

Tips for Responding to Essay Questions

1. Make sure your response is organized the way the question is organized.

If the question has four parts, write your answer in four parts, in the same order as they appear in the question. Do not simply start writing and have a continuous flow of rhetoric if the question is divided in parts. It is much easier for an instructor to evaluate your response if your question is organized appropriately.

2. Respond to what is requested.

One of the common mistakes students make with essay questions is not responding to what the question has asked for. Some students just start writing without trying to organize the points related to the question. Two techniques can help overcome this tendency: (1) Make a brief outline of the points you think are related. Then number the points in order of importance or relationship to the topic. (2) Use the *dumping* technique: Simply "dump out" all the ideas and facts you know by jotting them down. Then organize those ideas and points by numbering or lettering them. It might seem to you that you are using valuable time in organizing a response to the question. That is true, but once you have organized your answer, you will write it in less time than it takes to organize as you write.

Pay attention to the verb used in the question. You may be asked to *analyze, relate, produce, derive, develop, compare, contrast, interpret, differentiate, estimate, infer, extrapolate, classify, judge, validate, argue,* and so on. Each of these verbs requires a specific response from you—you can't just write what you know on the topic. If, for example, you are asked to *compare* two ideas, you must discuss how those ideas are alike, not how they are different. If you are asked to *analyze*, you must break the material into its component parts. If you are asked to *judge*, you must evaluate the material against criteria. Read questions carefully and pay attention to what the verb tells you to do.

3. Make sure you communicate effectively.

Sometimes students know material but communicate so poorly that the instructor can't determine if the correct information is contained in the response. If you don't write well without having a chance to rewrite, use short, simple sentences.

4. Try to make your handwriting legible.

Often you are writing rapidly and don't think to pay attention to the legibility of your handwriting. There is little more frustrating to an instructor than trying to read unreadable handwriting. Poor handwriting gives the instructor a negative mental set for evaluating your work properly. Print if your handwriting is difficult to read or write on every other line of the paper to make it easier to read.

5. Use correct grammar, spelling, and punctuation.

You may have grown accustomed to having only English teachers evaluate the mechanics of your writing. That may not be the case in college, where many instructors deduct points if a response contains glaring grammatical errors. Be careful with commas, because a misplaced comma can change the meaning of a sentence. You should take special care to spell correctly those words that are technical terms or are functionally related to the content, because using and spelling these words correctly indicate that you have some familiarity with the content.

6. Pay attention to the relative value of a question or parts of a question.

If an essay question has three parts and points are assigned to each part, don't spend an inordinate amount of time on a part that does not count much. Likewise, if an exam consists of four questions, notice the points assigned for each and put your time and emphasis on those that count the most.

7. Use key words and technical terms related to the subject.

Each subject has its own jargon. This jargon consists of the specific and technical terms that identify the subject and set it apart from another subject. Use those specialized terms in your answer—in your topic sentence, if possible. You will not only probably write a better response if you use the specialized language of the subject, but your instructor will know that you studied.

Sample Essay Questions

Here a few examples of essay questions and a description of what each asks for may be helpful.

1. The U.S. Constitution provides for the separation of powers. Describe what this means and why the framers of the Constitution included this provision. In your opinion, should that provision be contained in the Constitution? Why or why not?

This question has four separate parts: (1) describing the meaning of the provision; (2) describing why the provision is there; (3) stating your opinion; (4) indicating your reasons for holding that opinion. As you can see, you must have a knowledge base as well as support for your opinion to answer this question adequately. To make it easier for you to respond and easier for the instructor to follow, number or letter the four parts of your response.

2. What were three methods used by women's suffrage movements in the United States to secure the vote for women? How were these different from the methods used in England? Which methods were the most effective?

This question calls for knowledge associated with two suffrage movements and how these movements differed. To contrast the two movements, you must know the methods both used. You must also know how effective the various methods were in securing the vote for women. You could make two columns, one headed "United States" and the other headed "England" and list the methods used under each. Then you could address their differences: For example, you might say that the movement in England made more use of violence than the U.S. movement did. Then you should comment on the effectiveness of each method for the situation in which it was used. Again, you could simply list the methods 1, 2, 3 and then use categories such as weak, average, or strong to evaluate the effectiveness of each method.

3. Some historians believe that a successful League of Nations might have prevented some of the problems in Europe between World Wars I and II. Some believe that if the United States had joined the League of Nations, the organization might have had more influence. What do you think might have happened differently in Europe if the League had been successful?

This question does not have a correct answer because it is speculative. Its purpose is to determine if you know the goals and accomplishments of the League of Nations and the events that happened in Europe between World War I and World War II. Then you are asked to relate the two in terms of how the League might have acted to impact or change the course of events. This question would be evaluated in terms of your knowledge of what the League did do and might have done in relation to specific events in Europe between the wars. This type of question calls for a strong knowledge base and a good ability to put facts and ideas together to form a new picture, even though a speculative one.

4. Using the criteria given in class for judging a novel, apply those criteria to the novel assigned for outside reading.

The structure of a novel can usually be analyzed according to plot, climax, character development, and other features. In this question your instructor is asking you to apply these criteria or rules of structure to a novel assigned as outside reading. Assuming that your instructor has previously outlined these criteria and supplied examples, you should have no problem answering the question. One simple way is to list each criterion separately, explaining how the novel adheres or does not adhere to this rule of structure.

POST-EXAM ANALYSIS

An exam should be a learning experience. Instructors who recognize and believe that exams are learning experiences will use them as a teaching tool after marking them. If the instructor does not go over the exam carefully in class, you can do any of a number of things.

1. Get an appointment to discuss the exam with the instructor. Your goal here is to learn what you did incorrectly, not challenge the instructor. For objective exams, ask for an explanation of the items you did not understand. For essay exams, try to find out why your answer was not well done.

2. Go over the questions you missed using your notes and the text. Dig out the answers to those missed questions and mentally put aside the incorrect responses or faulty thinking. Recite the correct responses or think through the information until you have thoroughly learned it, because you may see it on another exam.

3. If you did well on the exam, read it over and think about the questions you answered correctly. Reading over your essay or associating the answer with the question (stem) will reinforce your knowledge and help you remember the information in the future.

Review

Exams may be stress producing and they certainly consume a large amount of time, but they are also very important to success in college. Your academic record is, to a large extent, a record of how well you performed on exams. Know what your strengths and weaknesses are in preparing for exams; build on the strengths and overcome the weaknesses. Develop a systematic procedure for study and follow that procedure. Study throughout the term rather than just a few days before an exam. If your study procedures are not successful or if you are not spending enough time with books, change your pattern immediately after your first poor performance. Finally, use your head during an exam. Don't make careless mistakes such as inadvertently omitting an answer. Don't walk away from an exam with the comment, "I knew that one — I just didn't think it through."

Review Questions

1. When should you begin preparing for an exam?
2. Have you developed a study strategy for exams?
3. Should you study differently for different types of exams?
4. What are mnemonic devices? Do you use them?
5. What kind of material should you memorize?
6. Why do instructors use essay exams?
7. What is a seductive alternative? Have you been trapped by one?
8. What are two tricks in responding to true/false questions?

For Further Reading

Farquar, William et al. *Learning to Study*. New York: Ronald Press, 1960.

Gilbert, Doris. *Study to Depth*. Englewood Cliffs, N.J.: Prentice-Hall, 1966.

Reutten, Mary. *Comprehending Academic Lectures*. New York: Macmillan, 1986.

TIME MANAGEMENT AS A KEY TO SUCCESS

N o doubt you've heard many complaints like this (perhaps you were the one doing the complaining): "Where does the day go? It seems like I just get started on something and bang!, the day's shot. I can't get anything done. The more I try to do and the harder I work, the further behind I get!"

Sound familiar? That one complaint is heard at colleges and universities with the same frequency as complaints about the cafeteria's food. It is especially prevalent during periods of accelerated activity: before mid-term exams, before due dates for term papers and projects, and before final exams. The whole school year is full of time pressure, but those pressures get especially severe at exam time and the end of term.

It is very human to complain about lack of time, but complaining does not help much. No matter how much or how loudly you complain, extra hours won't be added to each day to help you out, nor will extra days be added to each week. Time spent complaining could be better invested in some other activity — including developing a plan that will allow you to meet your goals, a plan that might eliminate the need for complaining about how much you can't accomplish.

All students moan and groan about time, but few take positive steps to ease and accommodate those pressures. This chapter is designed to make you aware of the importance of effective time management, of the many steps you can take to prevent your having to suffer the frustrations of "not enough time."

* * * * * * * * * *

THE FASTER I RUN, THE FARTHER I FALL BACK IN THE RACE!

* * * * * * * * * *

ESTABLISHING PRIORITIES

The first step in managing your time more efficiently is to list all your activities throughout the week. After all, until you see how and where you spend your time, it will be impossible to develop any type of plan to make better use of that time. Place a checkmark by each of the activities you spend your time doing:

_____ working

_____ volunteer activities

_____ studying

_____ attending classes

_____ researching/copying materials in the library

_____ writing papers and project reports

_____ reading—both for school and for pleasure

_____ shopping

_____ leisure activities (watching TV, hobbies, sports, etc.)

_____ family commitments

_____ "lifestyle" activities (haircuts, car repairs)

_____ travel (to and from work, school, and leisure activities)

_____ sleeping

_____ "goofing off"

Once you've worked through this checklist, you might be surprised to find how many different ways your time is spent throughout a normal week. You'll probably see that only two or three items (at most) are *not* checked off!

Few college students spend all their time simply going to college; you have many other responsibilities and activities that devour your time off campus. The challenge you face is organizing your time in such a way that you can fulfill your many life commitments and responsibilities without losing your mind in the process. Several years ago, it was fashionable in corporate America to engage in "time-and-task" analyses to determine how long it took to complete a certain task. You might find it useful to see exactly how much time you actually spend doing the many things you do every day. You may find a lot more time gets used up in various activities than you realized.

To understand where your time goes, let's examine some of those activities on your checklist to see how they might affect your weekly time expenditures.

• • • • • • • • •

IF I KNEW WHERE IT WENT, I MIGHT BE ABLE TO FIND IT!

• • • • • • • • •

A generation ago, it was fairly common for most college students to go to school without having to work at the same time. College costs were much lower then, and loan and grant monies were readily available, thereby allowing most students the luxury of being able to devote most of their energies and time to simply being a student. The cost of tuition, fees, room and board, and textbooks has skyrocketed dramatically during the past twenty years, however, making higher education an expensive commodity indeed. At the same time, it has become increasingly harder to get financial aid to offset those costs. The typical American college student has been caught in the middle of this squeeze. More and more students have found they must work, at least part time, to make ends meet. One 1986 study found that nearly three-fourths of all college freshmen work at least part time, with nearly 40 percent working sixteen hours or more each week to help meet expenses. If you find you must work to be able to attend college, that work commitment must be an important priority in trying to structure a reasonable schedule.

The amount of time you spend in a classroom and studying outside class will, of course, be affected by the number and type of classes you take each term and by your particular study habits. Though it's impossible to calculate an accurate number of hours you'll spend in a classroom, the average full-time student spends at least twelve hours in class each week, and perhaps as many as eighteen hours. Additionally, you should expect to spend at least two hours per week outside class studying for *each* class, and that is probably a bare minimum. More advanced and complex classes (computer science, for example) will require much more out-of-class time to complete the appropriate amount of studying. Being a successful student *is* a full-time job.

• • • • • • • • • •

WHY CAN'T THEY INVENT A THIRTY-HOUR DAY?

• • • • • • • • • •

Other school-related time commitments such as researching, doing supplementary reading, and writing papers place additional burdens upon your time, especially during certain parts of each academic term. Because most professors require that term papers or projects be completed and handed in during the last few weeks of school, you can bet that time will be tighter for you then — at the same time you're trying to study for final examinations. Most students feel the greatest pressure near the end of the term, when all course-related responsibilities (papers, projects, and final exams) come due at roughly the same time. That's why students (perhaps you) have found it necessary to pull "all-nighters" to get everything done at the end of the term.

You'll also find that your typical week is consumed by all kinds of non-work and nonschool commitments, ranging from the important (grocery shopping) to the relatively unimportant (getting a haircut), but every one of those activities takes a bite out of your time. If you are married and have children, these additional responsibilities will be even more severe and demanding.

Finally, you ought to realize that you'll spend time (a lot more time than you think) each week doing nothing, or "goofing off." That does not mean this is time ill spent. On the contrary, everyone needs time to relax, to do nothing, to simply take some time to recharge batteries. No one can keep going full speed all the time, so those moments of doing nothing in particular can be vitally important to your overall physical and mental health — as long as you don't spend most of your time in this area!

Here's that time checklist again, but this time try to estimate how much of your time each week you spend for/on each activity:

ACTIVITY	TIME SPENT/WEEK
Working	
Volunteer Activities	
Studying	
Attending Classes	
Researching/Copying Materials	
Writing Papers/Projects	
Reading	
Shopping	
Leisure Activities	
Family Commitments	
Lifestyle Activities	
Travel	
Sleeping	
"Goofing Off"	

If you experienced difficulty in trying to recall the amount of time spent on each activity, you might want to keep track of what you do with your time for the next week or so. Many, if not most, people actually are unaware of how they do spend their time, and sometimes filling in a checklist like you just did can be very revealing. Then they can say, "Now I *know* why I can't get everything done I want to!" Perhaps you had the same reaction.

Once you have determined how your week is spent, then you need to see if you are spending your time wisely and appropriately. Just because you spend a lot of your time on one activity doesn't mean that you *should* spend that much time on that activity. Now you need to establish priorities.

Go back to that checklist again. After reexamining each of the listed activities, place a number by each one in order of decreasing importance. Put a number 1 by the most important activity, 2 by the second most important, and so on. Now compare your numbers with the amount of time you spend on each activity. If your priorities are in order, the activity listed as 1 should have the greatest amount of time devoted to it. If, however, you find substantial disparities between the importance you assign to the activity and the time allotted to it, then you need to rethink the priority you gave to that activity. If you have found that you are one of those people who "don't have enough time" and you have been honest in completing the checklist, some disparity should show up that partially explains the problem you have. Your ninth most important activity should not consume the second greatest amount of time you spend each week.

To help establish your priorities, you need to determine what is of greatest importance to you at this time. Because you are in college, it is obvious that those activities relating to school are, or should be, very important to you, and those activities must be given high priority in putting together a workable time plan. It is easy to cut classes and not to give enough time to your studies, but you will be the one to suffer in the end. If you are going to be a college student and you want to be successful in that role, then you must reorient your schedule to provide for those necessities. It is easy to cut that biology or history class, but your grades and your future career may suffer ultimately. To be a student means that you must make being a student a high priority in your life.

DEVELOPING A REALISTIC SCHEDULE

Once you've determined your priorities, figuring out where you need to place the appropriate amounts of your time on a weekly basis, the next task is to develop a clearly defined schedule. This schedule, which must be flexible enough to handle unforeseen circumstances, you should view as a blueprint for accomplishing your many goals.

• • • • • • • • • •

A SCHEDULE IS A BLUEPRINT FOR GOAL ACHIEVEMENT.

• • • • • • • • • •

If you want to succeed in college, then you must develop a schedule to achieve that goal; if you need to work part time to meet expenses while going to school, then you must adjust your schedule to be able to achieve both goals simultaneously. Overall, it is most essential that your schedule be realistic, that you can reasonably meet the demands it places on you. If, however, you put together an impossibly crowded, unrealistic schedule, the demands created by that schedule may prove to be worse than the frustration caused by having no schedule at all.

• • • • • • • • • •

A REALISTIC SCHEDULE IF NECESSARY FOR YOUR SANITY.

• • • • • • • • • •

Let's start to develop a schedule for you by noting the most important elements that will consume the largest amounts of your time:

Attending Class. How many hours per week should you expect to find yourself in the classroom? In coming up with this number, remember to include any laboratory time so that the final figure will be the *maximum* amount of time you'll be in class. This is a commitment you don't want to cheat, because your being in class will result in your having better grades. Outside studying will not make up for cutting classes.

HOURS IN CLASS/WEEK: _____

Studying. Based on your past study habits as well as your plans to improve your study habits, how many hours a week will you spend studying? At a minimum, you should plan to spend two hours studying each week for each class.

HOURS STUDYING/WEEK: _____

Other School-Related Activities. Realistically, how much time per week will you be engaged in writing papers, doing additional research and reading beyond normal classroom expectations, working on projects, and the like? Remember to include the amount of time you will spend in the library and computer center in carrying out these additional activities.

HOURS IN SCHOOL – OUT-OF-CLASS ACTIVITIES/WEEK: _____

Working. Is it necessary for you to work to go to school? Does your job have normal, weekly work hours, or are you "on call" at widely different hours? In trying to determine your weekly job commitment, don't forget to include the time it takes to travel to and from the job site.

HOURS WORKING/WEEK: _____

Family Activities. Calculate the amount of time you must spend with your family, an especially important area if you are married and have small children. Just as you do not want to shirk school or job responsibilities, you certainly don't want to shirk those all-important family responsibilities. Besides, they give you excellent physical and mental relief from the rigors of academic life.

HOURS WITH FAMILY/WEEK: _____

Other Personal Responsibilities/Activities. This is a broad category of miscellaneous activities, including personal hygiene (doing laundry, getting haircuts) and leisure activities. If you've made a commitment with some friends to play racquetball twice a week, count that in your time calculations, including travel, play, and (hopefully) showering. Though it may appear that you're only going to play for one hour, you'll probably spend a total of two hours when you add the time spent getting dressed to play, taking a shower, and then getting dressed to leave. Many of our personal activities take much more time than we initially realize.

HOURS PERSONAL/WEEK: ⎯⎯⎯⎯

Rest and Relaxation. As we noted earlier, you'll spend some time "goofing off" each week, primarily relaxing and doing nothing. Plus, unless you're Superman or Supergirl, you'll need to spend time sleeping to recharge your body physically and mentally. In calculating this time, don't short yourself on the amount of sleep you need. No one knows your body or your body's needs better than you, so don't be misled by others who claim you only need a certain number of hours of sleep each night. You might need less than that, or more, but only you really know. If you want to perform successfully in college, you'll want to get the appropriate amount of rest your body needs.

HOURS R&R/WEEK: ⎯⎯⎯⎯

Now look over the number of hours you've calculated. If you've done a good job of analyzing your activities, you should be able to see how your overall schedule needs to be organized. By establishing priorities for your time, then estimating an overall schedule to accommodate those priorities, you can now move on to the development of a weekly plan that will meet your needs.

• • • • • • • • • •

ONCE I SEE ALL THE PARTS, THE WHOLE FINALLY MAKES SENSE!

• • • • • • • • • •

FOLLOWING THE PLAN

At this point, you've determined how you presently spend your time, what your priorities should be, and how much time you should allot to each of your different activities and responsibilities. Now you need to put together an actual plan to make the pieces fit together, a plan that meets your needs yet is flexible enough to handle changing situations and demands. It is time to develop a cohesive weekly schedule for managing your time.

By reexamining the different time commitments you noted earlier, complete this chart, fitting in your commitments as they are most appropriate. For example, if you have an American History class that meets from 9–10 a.m. on Monday, Wednesday, and Friday, then make that notation in the 9:00 a.m. slot on those three days of the week. Do the same for every other commitment, leaving nothing out of your time commitment list. Now you can easily visualize what your weekly schedule should look like, and you can move some of your commitments around so that you're not overloaded on just two or three days.

YOUR WEEKLY PLAN

	Monday	Tuesday	Wednesday	Thursday	Friday	Saturday	Sunday
8:00 a.m.							
9:00 a.m.							
10:00 a.m.							
11:00 a.m.							
NOON							
1:00 p.m.							
2:00 p.m.							
3:00 p.m.							
4:00 p.m.							
5:00 p.m.							
6:00 p.m.							
7:00 p.m.							
8:00 p.m.							
9:00 p.m.							
10:00 p.m.							

Notice a couple of things about your plan chart. First, there are no slots for the 11:00 p.m. hour or later. Even if you take college classes at night, they tend to be completed before 10 p.m., so there is no need to take the schedule later. Additionally, most college student work schedules are completed before 10 p.m., but if you happen to be one of the few working the "graveyard shift" while going to college, you can make the necessary modifications to the chart.

Second, notice that your plan includes all seven days of the week, not just the five working days of Monday through Friday. You need to include the weekend days of Saturday and Sunday in planning for study time, writing papers, working, personal and family commitments, and so on. Those weekend days can be very important in helping to lighten the load of the other five days. So, if your analysis of nonsleep commitments totaled, say, 80 hours, you can spread that time across seven days, not just five.

Once you have completed your personal plan chart, you have a viable time blueprint for successful time management. Now you have to stick to your plan. This plan is only going to work if you are willing to follow it. Granted, situations arise that will cause you to modify the plan every now and then, but if those exceptions become the rule, then you really have no plan at all.

Your plan is very much like a road map, an indicator of how you may steer a success course through your various commitments and responsibilities. Follow that plan!

TWO FINAL THOUGHTS

Although your schedule makes each time of day look the same as every other, that is really not the case, especially in regard to your study time. You need to assess your own habits/predispositions about appropriate times to study. For example, some students prefer studying a subject immediately after class; others want time to "get away" from that class before studying the material. Neither way is right nor wrong; the decision about when to study is very personal. The main point is: *You must make a conscious decision to study when that time is best for you.*

A second thought on rest and diet: Because you will spend many hours each week studying, you want to spend those hours as profitably as possible. Getting the right amount of rest is important to effective study habits, as is proper diet. Your body requires proper rest and nourishment, and the effectiveness of your study time will be affected by those two factors. So, as Mom and Dad told you for those many years, eat properly and get enough rest — and you'll receive benefits of improved QUALITY study time.

 Review

Many college students have great difficulty in trying to fit their varied commitments and responsibilities into their time schedules. It is important to take an active approach towards time management: (1) determine what your commitments and responsibilities are, (2) determine the appropriate priorities for spending your time, (3) calculate the amount of time needed each week to meet your commitments and responsibilities, and (4) develop a carefully prepared plan for alloting your time throughout a full seven-day week.

Once you've developed your plan for time management, stick to it.

Review Questions

1. Time management can mean a lot to the successful college student. Try this little test: Have you noticed how the better students in your classes manage their time? Do they seem to have a plan for meeting their objectives? (We bet they do.)

2. Once you've completed and followed your personal plan, were you surprised to find how "much more time" you seemed to have at your disposal? In which areas did that "extra" time appear?

3. Have your grades been positively affected by your time plan? If you stick to your plan and it is a realistic one, your grades will probably show improvement.

4. Do you feel more in command of things and less frustrated with a time

plan to follow? Do you intend to do similar planning once you leave school and embark on your career?

5. Isolate the greatest changes in your time spent — before and after developing your time plan. Where have you made your greatest gains?

For Further Reading

McGregor, Douglas. *The Human Side of Enterprise*. New York: McGraw-Hill, 1960.

INDEX